Refuge Cove
Coastal Kitchen

This book is dedicated to my husband John. Our expeditions began fifteen years ago sailing up to Refuge Cove along with my son Ben. We stopped in to visit with John's childhood friends. Every year the adventures continue. Live with great expectations and wondrous events will unfold.

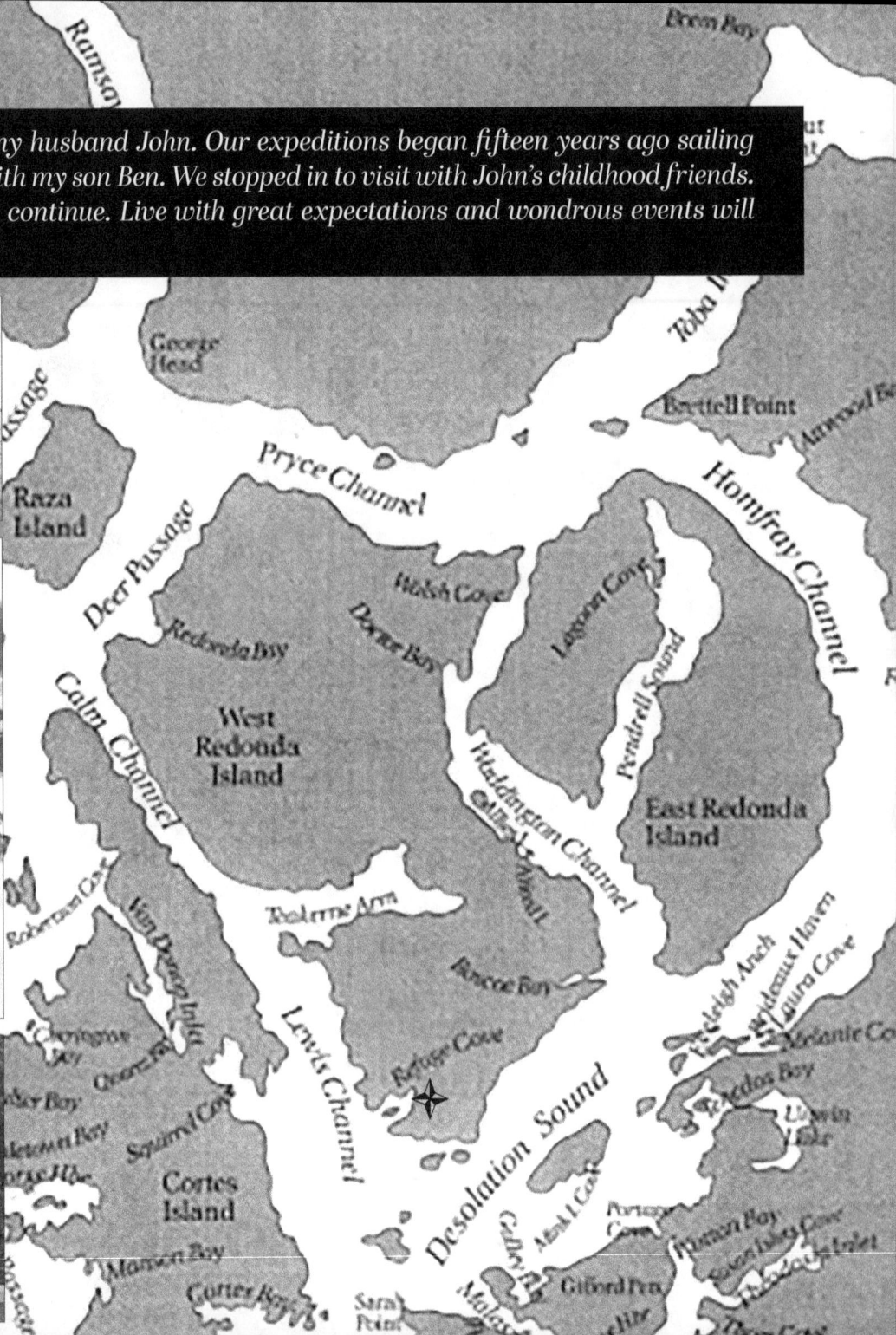

Library and Archives Canada Cataloguing in Publication

Refuge Cove Coastal Cookbook : recipes & historical stories

Desolation Sound B.C. / Cathy Jupp Campbell.

ISBN 978-0-9879968-0-0

1. Cooking. 2. Cookbooks--History.

I. Jupp Campbell, Cathy, 1954-

TX714.R445 2012 641.5 C2012- 901916-X

Art by Judith Williams, Mary Ruzich and Meghan Paterson
Photographs and sketches by Cathy Jupp Campbell
Typeset in Abril at SpicaBookDesign.
Printed in Victoria, B.C. Canada

Refuge Cove Coastal Kitchen

Refuge Cove Land and Housing Cooperative

In the Heart of Desolation Sound, British Columbia, Canada

Recipes and Coastal Stories

Refuge Cove is a unique boardwalk community, a small coastal settlement tucked away on Redonda Island in Desolation Sound. People cruising the salt chuck have been coming to Refuge Cove to stock up with fresh food and provisions since the early 1900's and still do to this day.

Refuge Cove has always been a shelter from the storm, serving boaters with essential amenities such as provisions from the Refuge Cove Store, a fully serviced fuel dock, secure moorage, Upcoast Summer Restaurant, Refuge Cove Gallery and Refuge Cove Sailing Charters.

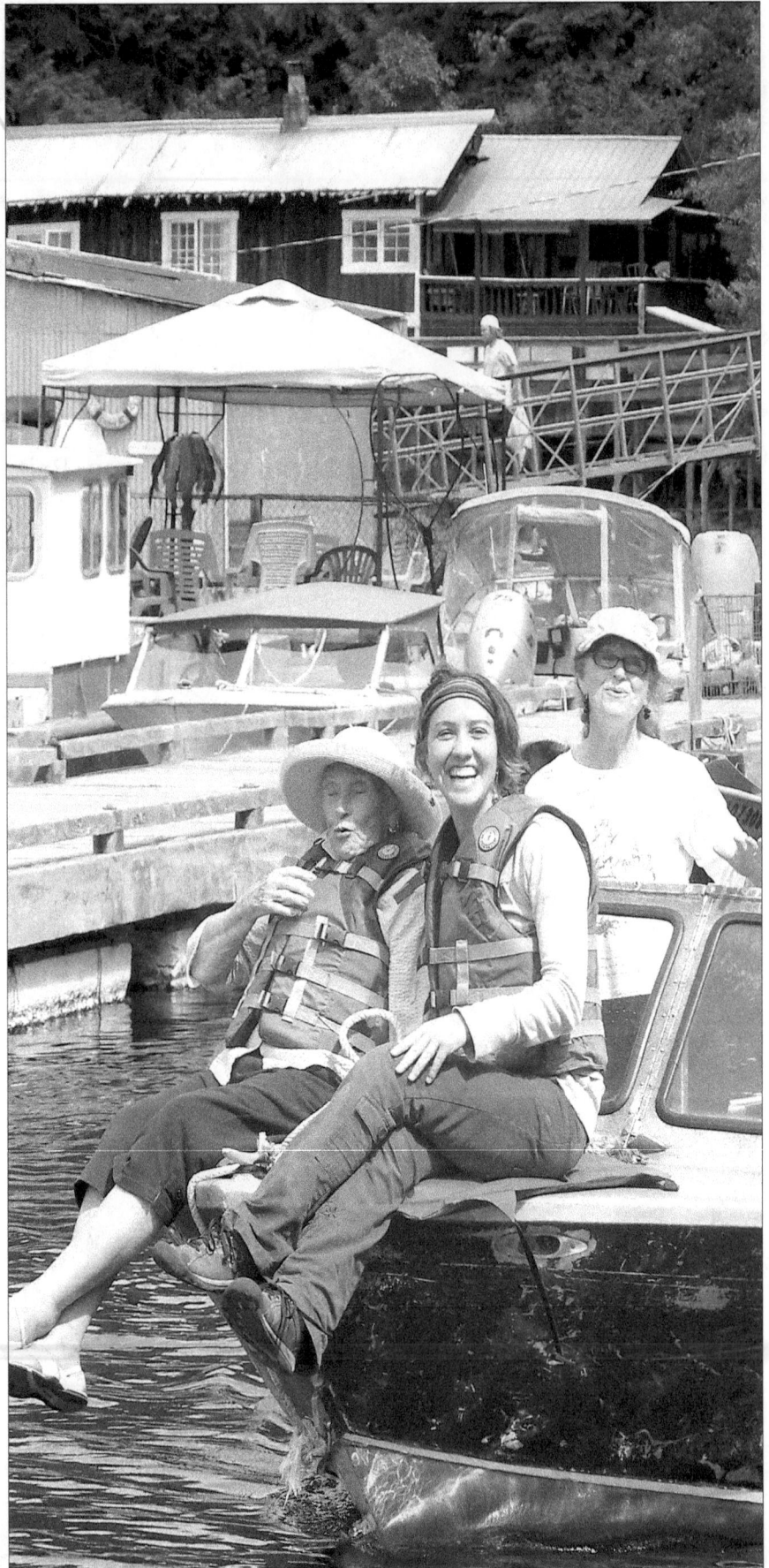

Meme.
Photo by Matt Dixon

Here is where the gathering of a community of friends and family was built, strong in their belief for an ideal lifestyle, blending work and play together with fairness and respect for each other.

Introduction

The recipes, short stories and photographs in this book are a compendium of the past 45 years and was originally made to commemorate the 40th Anniversary of Refuge Cove Land and Housing Cooperative. This book is a second edition revised for the Refuge Cove Exhibition at Cortes Island Museum in 2017. The wonderful stories, art and images were submitted by the members and friends of Refuge Cove in Desolation Sound, British Columbia.

Special acknowledgements to Denise Gibbons, Lena Johnson and Frieda Home for the archival photographs & recipes and to Judith Williams for images of her paintings, recipes, photographs and stories. Thanks to Mary Ruzich for her fabric art and Meghan Patterson for her paintings. Your contributions have been the yeast that has given rise to bind the fibers of this book together. I hope you enjoy the tongue and cheek humour, a prerequisite for the stories told. Thanks to all Refugees for your oral and written stories and your enthusiasm in making this book tangible.

It has been such an honor to meet and spend time with such a creative and gifted group of wonderful people. I value our summer family and all the memorable experiences shared here.

Photography, book designing & editing Cathy J. Campbell

"All the groceries for the store arrive by freight and are moved by an ingenious motorized (model A engine) track from the dock to the store where the boxes were unloaded into the stock room."

Anne Ferguson
1970's

Now the staff from the store take the herring skiff across Lewis Channel to the Squirrel Cove dock. They unload the freight truck that has delivered food and supplies from Vancouver Island. They time the tides high so the ramp isn't to steep from the dock to the skiff.

"The real voyage of discovery consists not in seeking new lands but in seeing with new eyes."

Proust

Downtown
Refuge Cove.

**Photo by
Cathy J Campbell**

There are many food stories of Refuge Cove, starting when we showed up there in May of 1965. Doris Hope was always glad to have an excuse to go fishing so she would throw an obscure cut (from the beef side hanging in the cooler) with a variety of vegetables into the slow oven of the oil stove and off we would go, leaving Norm and Ken to mind the store while we caught cod and salmon.

Once when Doris had gone to Vancouver and we arrived to work on our boat on the (Blacks) ways in the Hole, Norm announced that he had received a goose from Galley Bay and expected me to cook it for dinner. I had never eaten goose, never mind cooked one, but into the oven it went with celery and onions and we had it for dinner. It was rather tough but washed down with the usual libations. We ate it all.

All the way along the coast on our first trip to Refuge Cove from Vancouver at 6 knots, people informed us that the meat purchased there was superior. We discovered that Hope Brothers Store Ltd. purchased extra aged beef sides and kept them in the cooler for at least another week before selling the cuts. We also discovered that we too were expected to make the desired cuts-after hoisting the side off the hook in the cooler and plunking it on the large cutting block in the store. The steaks were wonderful-cut thick and bar-bequed. Doris was fond of a shell bone roast. Doris and Norm also butter flied lamb for customers upon request. We all lived very well with lots of seafood at hand too. We had memorable times!

All the groceries for the store arrived by freight and were moved by an ingenious motorized (model A engine) track from the dock to the store where the boxes were unloaded into the stock room. When the fresh stuff arrived the store was closed until it had been dealt with, often with the assistance of the waiting customers.

When the Cooperative purchased Refuge Cove, after the fire, after Hope's barge purchase, after the repossession, people arrived to live in Refuge Cove and we had many wonderful potluck meals and community Christmas dinners.

One year one of the turkeys was cooked in a mustard paste. Some of the turkey, paste and all, was consumed with no apparent negative effect.

Doris and Norm were delighted to have a community again. The Christmas dinners and other celebrations were held at their home for many years.

Story by Anne Ferguson

Joan Carter's first trip to see her Auntie Doris and Uncle Norman Hope was on the Union Steamship Chelohsin in the summer of 1945 with the captain who gave her the opportunity of steering the boat. Later she remembers trips up on the Gulf Stream and Gulf Wing Ships. She was put to work by Auntie Doris stocking shelves in the Refuge Cove Store.

"There were always big parties in the schoolhouse or up at the lake on the little island. I remember barbeques and bonfires, open fire cooking, sing songs and dancing. If I sat quietly in a corner I could listen to all the gossip I wasn't supposed to hear. Oh, of course that was after they had a few drinks. I lived to get away to Refuge to be with my surrogate parents Doris and Norman Hope."

This famous picture of Doris and Norm Hope "the Duke and Duchess of West Redonda" & their dog Stinky, late 1940's.

In 1918 the Donley Trading Company was established on West Redonda Island in Desolation Sound, one hundred miles north of Vancouver. In 1945 Doris and Norm Hope purchased the buildings, docks and 186 acres of land from Jack Tindall, who had owned it for 15 years. In 1972, 18 shareholders formed The Refuge Cove Land and Housing Co-op on the Hopes' acres. "We did not so much buy a piece of land as invest our futures in a tangled web of west coast history."

From Judith Williams book, *Dynamite Stories*

Contents

Recipes

Stories

Helpful Hints

from Auntie Doris

Doris helped run Joyce Point Logging which they owned just north of Teakerne Arm up Lewis Channel.

Aggie and George worked with Doris & Norm Hope.

They lived in Mel & Lena's place. George was a fisherman and Aggie was a camp cook.

Aggie taught Doris how to catch fish.

She would sit down the *'Green Girls of the Woods'* and seriously express her theories to them.

1. Stale cookies and crackers at the store were crisped up in the oven to use. One mustn't let anything go to waste.

2. When reheating sliced roast beef, put lettuce on top of it to keep it moist.

3. Elastic bands around a spoon would keep it from falling in the stew pot.

4. Freshen dried onion, red and green pepper, fruits and herbs by soaking for 20 minutes in warm water to cover. Drain and use.

5. When making jelly, 1 tbsp. Epsom salts to 5 lbs. of fruit will take the place of commercial pectin.

6. Freeze limes, lemons and oranges for easy zesting.

7. Add baking soda to green beans when steaming to keep them bright green.

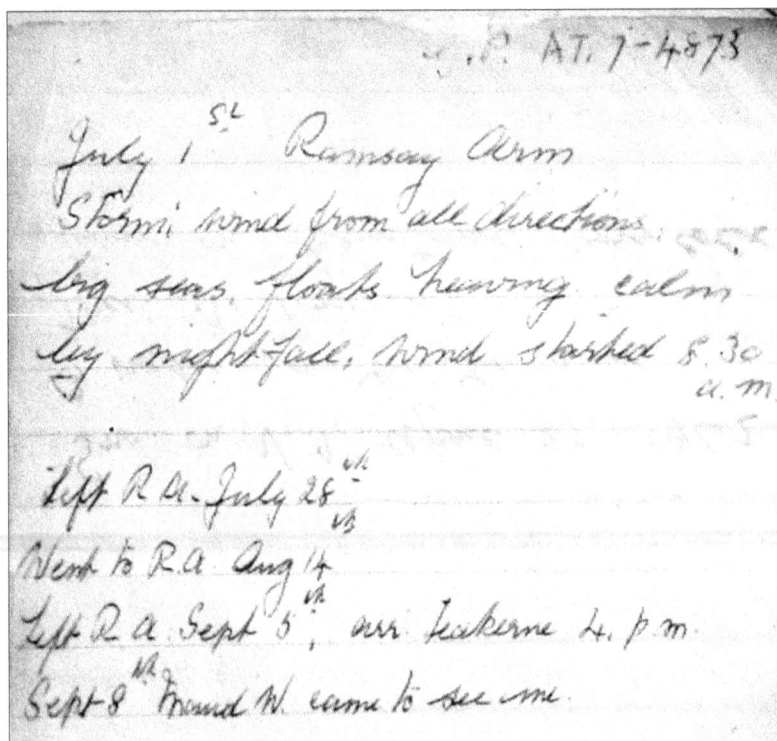

Dorothy Thomas's notes on steno pad.

Breakfast and Breads

Watercolour painting by Judith Williams

John Campbell is known fondly as "The Prawn King of Refuge Cove."

From spring to autumn, they industriously set out for the daily hunt for prawns.

There are many stories to tell about their prawn pulling adventures by folks who have had the opportunity to venture out with them.

This picture is of John in John Dixon's handsome lifeboat with a new white prawn puller.

The old prawn puller was on the bow. It was a pot puller from Alaska with a Briggs and Stratton engine.

It was very dangerous to operate because it only ran at high speed and if the line snagged it would jam up in the pulley.

You can also use a prawn puller for heavier articles that might come up with your prawn traps such as old ice boxes, bed springs and the like.

Many traps and pullers have been lost in their conquests over the years.

Prawns on Eggs with Cheese Toast Fry

Fresh prawns headed & shelled & boiled for 2 minutes max.

Fry an **egg** sunny side up in bacon fat

Fry **toast** in bacon fat or butter

Place egg on top of toast in pan

Add a layer of thinly sliced **cheddar cheese**

Place **prawns** on top of cheese

Continue cooking on medium heat until cheese is melted. Place hot sauce and chili sauce on table. Serve individually to at least half a dozen waiting customers at the table on the boat. Season to own taste with hot sauce and salt and pepper.

John L. Campbell, MV *Evening Star One*

Reinhold is an apiarist at Refuge Cove and on Cortes Island
He has been a bee keeper for many years.
The honey he collects from his colonies is the sweetest treat
around Desolation Sound. The smoker in the picture
belonged to Reinhold's father Ernie.
It is late summer and he is feeding
the bees.

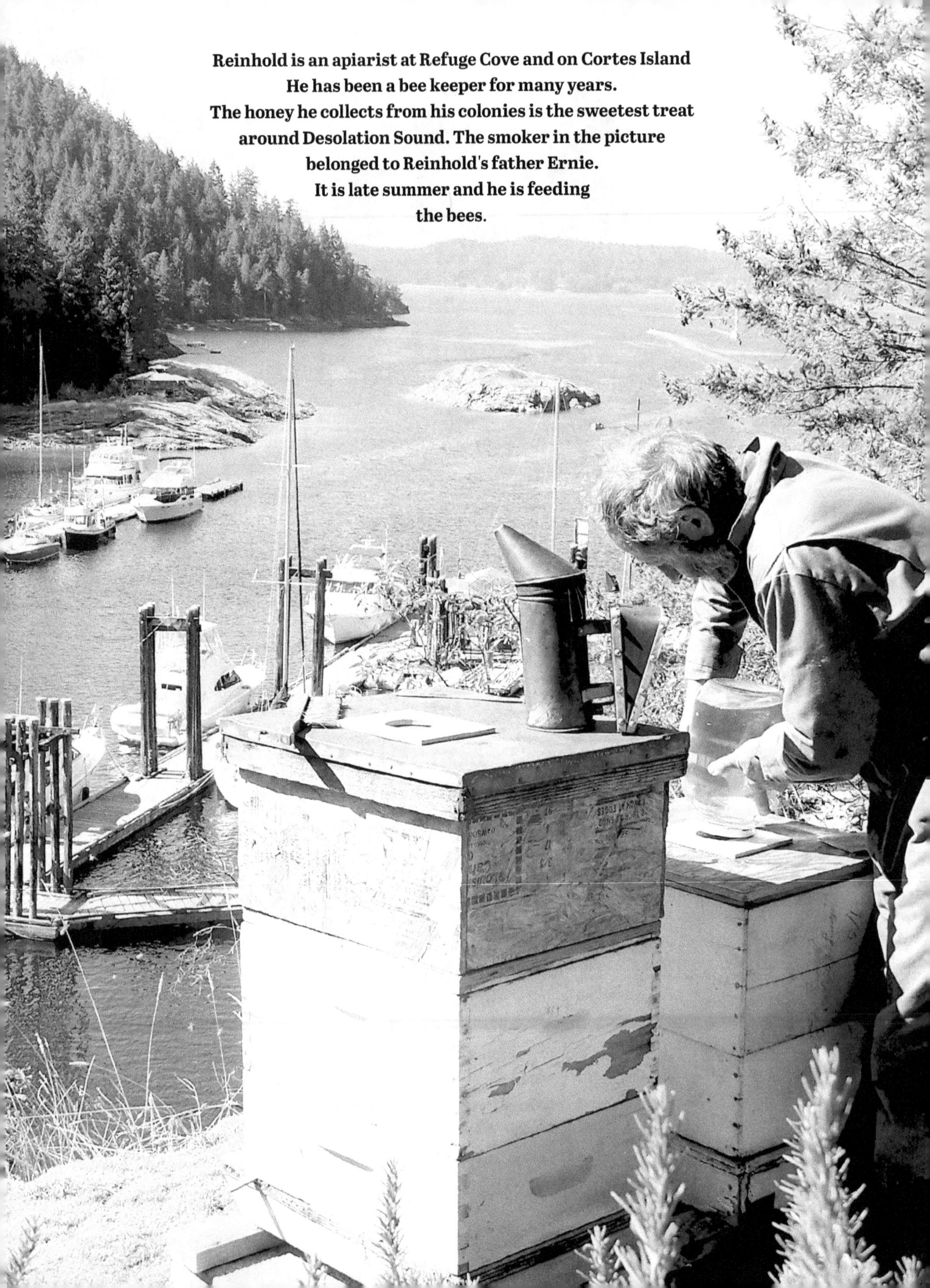

Reinhold's Pancakes

4 cups **oatmeal**

1 litre **buttermilk**

Mix together. Let sit over night in fridge.

Beat 4 **eggs** (5)

Add to mixture.

Add

1/2 cup **whole wheat flour** to

1 tbsp. **baking soda**

Add

1 cup **raisins**, a handful of **almond flakes, sesame, pumpkin, sunflower & poppy seeds**.

Make pancakes. Drizzle with **honey**.

Reinhold Hoge, the master apiarist of Desolation Sound was renowned for his hamburger stand for years and is now famous for his liquid gold honey. If you find a well groomed & well marked out trail, it was most likely made by Hoge.

Spruce Tip Syrup

Pick young twigs and tips from the spruce tree.

Wash then add 3 times the amount of sugar, a little water and boil down until it forms syrup.

Adjust to your taste.

Make a tea with tips with boiling water.

High in Vitamin C

There is an amusing story in Judith Williams "Dynamite Stories" about Bobo's dilemma delivering five keeper hives loaded with 300,000 bees in his car on a ferry to Cortes Island.

Hanne's Quiche Lorraine

We all enjoyed entertaining with many fine meals. Every day during the summer, there was another spectacular dinner in the making. We'd take turns, impressing each other with elaborate presentations and delicious food.

Fresh from the ocean was the gift of salmon, lingcod, snapper, scallops, clams, mussels & oysters.

From the land there was venison, bear, quail and other small creatures.

Colin Robertson recalls a time long ago when a farmer rowed all the way to Refuge Cove from Cortes Island to sell his eggs to the store. People would also bring fresh produce to sell. This was a long, long time ago.

Make dough for quiche. Use a greased spring form pan. (See column at right)

- 1-2 small **cooking onions**
- 250 g **bacon** cut in small pieces
- 6 **eggs**
- 1/2 litre **whipping cream**
- 150 g **Emmentaler cheese**
- 150 g **Gruyere cheese**

Slice onions paper thin.

Arrange single layer without gaps on bottom of crust.

Cut bacon and heat in frying pan (do not let it overcook)

Drain grease and let bacon cool on a piece of paper towel.

Distribute bacon on top of the onion layer.

Vigorously stir eggs with the whipping cream adding salt and pepper.

Grate both cheeses and add to the egg/cream mixture. Distribute this mixture with a ladle over the bacon and onion layers.

Bake in oven 350°F for 45 minutes until golden brown. Turn off oven and let pie settle somewhat.

Drinks: Serve hot with a dry white wine preferably Gewürztraminer.

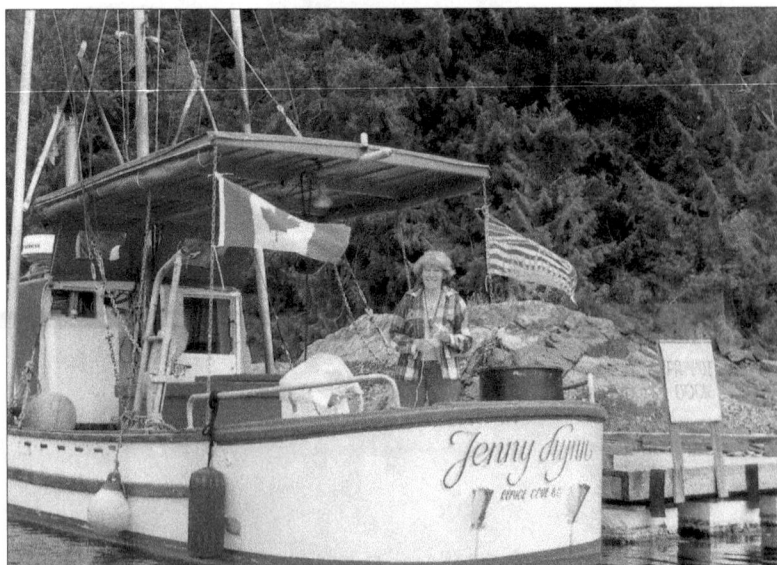

Hanne's Sauerkraut Quiche

Make Dough for Quiche. Used a greased spring form pan.

FILLING INGREDIENTS:

- 1 small cooking **onion** chopped finely
- 1 **apple** peeled cored and thinly sliced
- 75 g **bacon** cubed and fried
- 1 can **sauerkraut** (520 g)
- 2 **juniper berries**
- 1/2—1 tsp **caraway seeds**
- 1 **bay leaf**, salt & pepper
- 1/8 litre of dry **white wine**
- 1/8 litre of **vegetable broth**
- 20 ml **kirsch** (optional)
- 200 g **whipping cream**
- 4 **eggs**
- 100 g **Emmentaler cheese** grated

In a frying pan, cook up the bacon, the onion and apple and let stew together for 5 minutes. Add sauerkraut, juniper, caraway seeds, bay leaf and a little salt and pepper

Add enough wine just cover the surface.

Cook approximate 20 minutes possibly adding more wine.

At end of cooking period add kirshwasser.

Let cool. Remove bay leaf and juniper berries.

Drain kraut mixture and distribute on to the dough in the spring form pan.

Mix cream and eggs and pour over the kraut.

Distribute cheese over top of the cream and egg mixture in the spring form pan.

Bake at 350° for 35 minutes.

Let settle a little in oven after turning it off.

Hanne Potocnik

Hanne's Dough for Quiche

- 50 g **flour**
- 125 g **butter** (firm)
- 60 ml **milk**
- 2 **egg yolks**
- **Salt** and **pepper**

Knead all ingredients for the crust to a smooth even dough. Let stand 30 minutes in refrigerator or cool place. Set oven temperature to 350°F (175°C)

Roll out dough and place into a greased spring form (26 cm)

Forming a rim on sides.

Important!

Poke dough several times with a fork.

Growing Up At Refuge Cove

When Cathy asked me to make a contribution to the Refuge Cove cookbook, I was immediately thrilled at the thought of putting down memories on paper; yet the months ticked by and I found it increasingly difficult to find the words. What would I write? How would I articulate that which seems so elusive, so fleeting, yet so much part of who I am – that source of my being today.

Lisa Gibbons and brother Michael at Refuge Cove. 1971.
Photos courtesy of Denise Gibbons

I now realize that I am who I am because of Refuge Cove – for good or bad. I moved there as a wee child, vividly full of life and wonder at the age of four in 1971, and progressed through my childhood until the age of sixteen, when I had to leave for high school with my brother, Michael. I see myself as a true "refugee", as we came to call ourselves.

These were undoubtedly the formative years in my life and the influences ran deep. They formed a sense of place and gave me a gift of community – in all it's glory, as well as the moments of hardship and disappointment. Most importantly, appreciation of the land itself remains the main character in my dreams today.....a particular trail to follow, an intimate knowledge of a perch on a bluff, a beloved rock, a soft green carpet of moss, a silent moment by my favorite arbutus tree....the early morning call of the loon coming out from the lagoon.

Food, of course, was the major theme for us at Refuge Cove, food and gathering together for the purpose of cooking, eating, laughing, sharing and generally forgetting the difficulties in our lives. The "potluck" became essential....it was our proxy for all other forms of entertainment and tradition.......food became our culture, our coffee house, our family dinner, our church.... our substitute for everything we had given up in the world outside.

Food became the core of our stories, the memories of which we all shared. I remember: salmon, red snapper, lingcod, oysters, clams, prawns (we had parties where all that was served was prawns...mountains of prawns and huge stinking piles of carcasses beside every person after the feast was done).

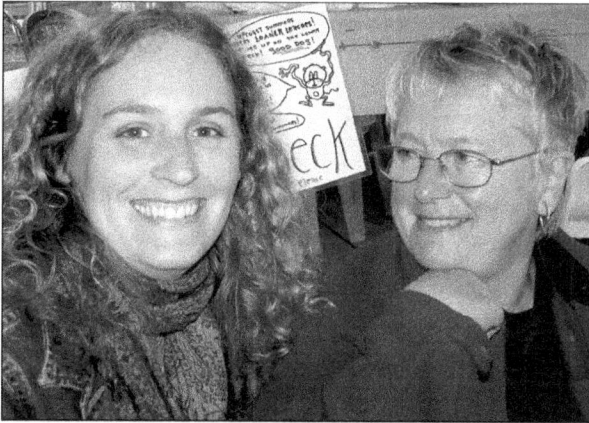
Lisa Gibbons with Judith Williams.

There are many vivid memories of the home-steader lifestyle too....dad dragging deer home, which mom would help cut up and prepare. Raising chickens, ducks and pigs and the pigs were an endless source of entertainment. One particular memory, after an exciting Christmas morning, Michael and I ventured out, me with my brand new Barbi and he, with my old, worn and oh-so-dated Barbi. He conceded to play the girl's game if I agreed to play his version, which meant they must be "adventure" Barbi's, complete with climbing ropes and attitude. So we set out to have our precious Barbi's scale the side of the pig pen and repel from the walls on precarious string ropes. In record time my new, beloved toy dropped into the pig pen and was instantly scooped up by a squealing pig, named Sir Francis Bacon. Sir Francis proceeded to run laps around the pen at full speed and all I could see of my doll was her two feet sticking out of his mouth! Catching the pig and wrestling my Christmas gift from his mouth is something I'll never forget. Poor Barbi never fully recovered and it was around that time I conceded that eating pork wasn't such a bad idea.

I also remember Christmas feast's at Auntie Doris and Uncle Norman's house and the "chicken plucker's stomp" at our house, where you had to pluck before you could partake in Mom's amaz-ing chicken dinner, followed by frenzied, all night dancing....there were potluck's on Center Island,

potluck's at the "school house".....and the "barge".... and of course, the famed "bear-bq" Halloween party where everyone was tricked after they had their treat of Dad's bear – stomach aches. Mom's Peking Duck party.....mom's sushi....mom's rock-fish cooked with chili's and hot sesame oil.....dad's Oyster's Rockefeller.....mom's chocolate cake...... mom's homemade bread with slices of dad's beef-steak tomatoes straight off the vine....fall's harvest of Chanterelles and Morels sautéed in the old pan with garlic and butter.

When I try to summon the best story or the most memorable food impression, what I come up with is the simplest and this is it ....Coming home from school, which, at the best of times was an excit-ing sail across Lewis Channel, and at the worst of times, was simply exhausting.....often dark, wet, cold, with a South-Easter blowing, patience running thin.....let's just say, sometimes, we were very, very grateful by the time we got home. The most wonderful part of returning to our warm house was being greeted by my loving parents and more often than not, my mom would have a nice hot pot of tea under the cozy, waiting just for us. Then she'd usually have a treat to go with it.....a bowl of popcorn with butter and yeast, or a new loaf of her famous Bannock right out of the cast iron fry pan.....or her lovely Welsh Griddle Cakes, which, went perfectly with a good cup of tea. This was the simple pleasure of coming home..... The love, the warmth, the nurtured feel-ing I received when I walked through the door is what has sustained me through all these years and inspired me to make sure my own children have that sense of knowing they are loved and knowing that they are *home*.

Lisa Gibbons

Lisa Gibbons Cortes Island artist, has been creating artwork for 25 years, using an array of mixed media techniques. She creates works that are multi-layered, evocative, mysterious and reflect her connection with the outer world as well as her inner landscape.

Cheesy Baked Dip

- 8 oz. **sour cream**
- 8 oz. **cream cheese**
- 16 oz. **cheddar cheese**, grated (sharp or mild)
- 4 oz. chopped **green chilies**
- **Green onion** (suit your own taste)
- 1 cup chopped **ham**
- 1/2 pound chopped **bacon**
- 1 round **bread loaf**, hollowed out

Mix first seven ingredients together and put into the hollowed out bread loaf.

Bake at 350°F uncovered for one hour.

Serve with leftover bread or chips.

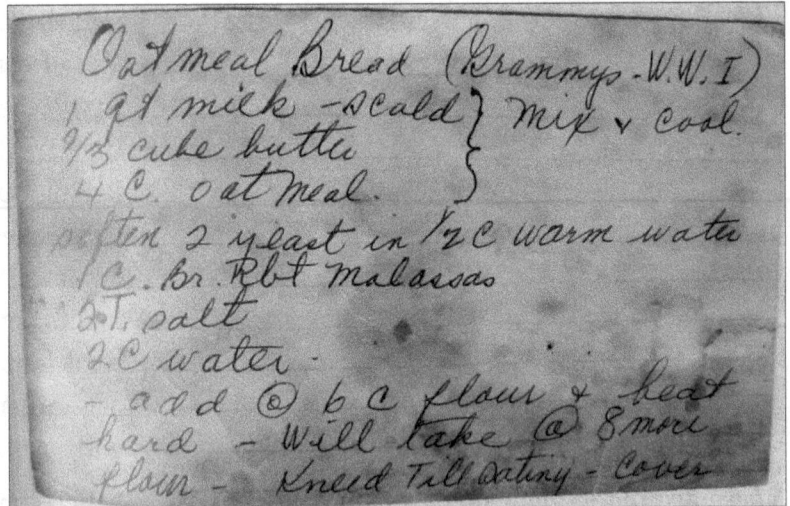

Recipe found in one of Doris Hope's recipe books at her boardwalk cabin.

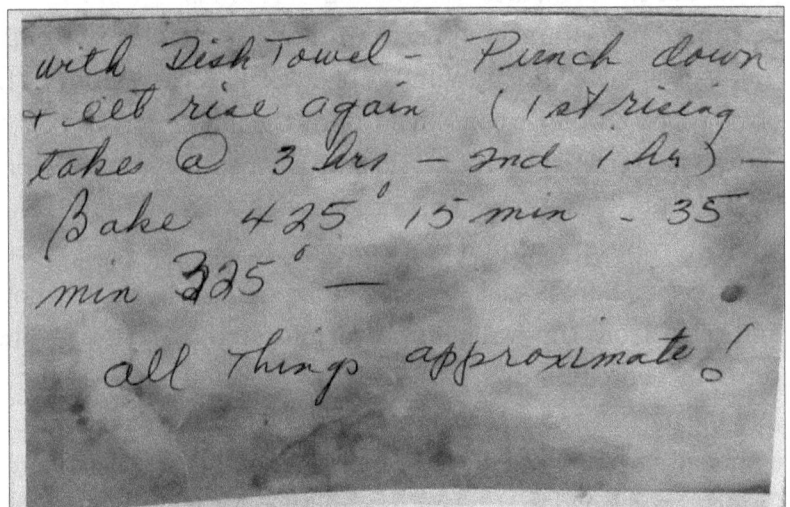

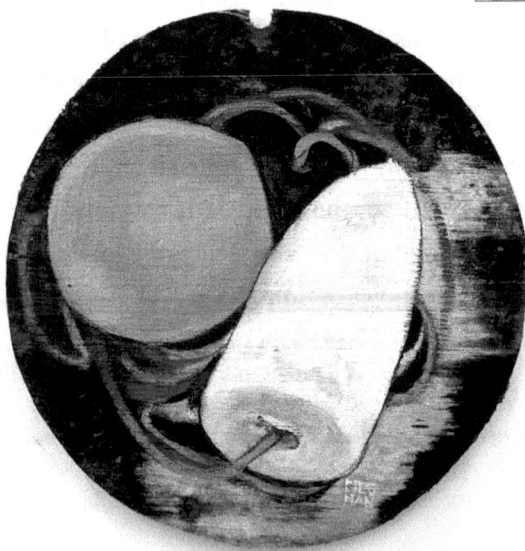

Einstein said: "Energy is equal to mass multiplied by the speed of light squared or E=mc2. For me E stands for our enjoyment from our energy, M stands for the meaning we give to life and c2 stands for the many ways of seeing. We are constantly falling apart and that is eventually how we get it all together."

Kids at Refuge Cove 1970's (left to right):
Dean Lovell, Michael Gibbons, Tracey Lovell, Lisa Gibbons & Lisa Hall.
Photo Courtesy of Lisa Gibbbons

Welsh Griddle Cakes

3 cups **flour**
1 1/2 tsp **baking powder**
1/2 tsp **baking soda**
1 1/4 tsp **salt**
1 cup granulated **sugar**
1 tsp **nutmeg**
1 cup **butter**
1 cup **currants**
2 **eggs**
6 tbsp **milk**
(more or less)

Sift dry ingredients in mixing bowl.

Cut in butter until small, crumbly texture.

Beat eggs and milk separately, then add to dry mixture.

Work with hands into a dough.

Roll out on floured surface and cut shapes out with knife or cookie cutters.

Cook in cast iron pan on low to medium heat.

When slightly puffed and brown, flip each cake over and cook other side until brown.

Eat warm and serve with butter, jam & honey or just enjoy plain.... yum.

Lisa Gibbons

Bannock

Combine 3 cups **flour**, a dash of salt 1 tsp **baking powder** in a bowl.

Make a little well and pour 2 tbsp **water** in it.

Mix into dough and knead.

Flatten it out and put in a frying pan in 2 tbsp of **lard**. Can also be made with mashed potatoes.

Oat Cakes

Combine
    2/3 cup fine **oatmeal**
    2/3 cup **flour**
    ¼ tsp **soda**
    ¼ tsp **baking powder**
    ¼ tsp **salt**

Mix together 1 tbsp melted butter with a dribble of hot water.

Add dry ingredients to make dough.

Roll out until thin and cut into quarters or use a glass to cut out circles.

Heat cast iron pan until drops of water dance on the surface and cook oatcakes until edges curl and toast.

They shouldn't brown.

Repeat on other side.

French Baguette Bread

Odysseus, the most saltcaked of ancient heroes is surely a companion of anyone who has felt the terror at the helm. A poem about the journey through the uncharted waters of one's life goes, "to live well in one's life in the world, you must stay with your ship, stay tied to the present, remain mobile, keep adjusting the rig, work with the swells, watch for the wind shift, watch as the boom swings over, engage in other words with the muddle and duplicity and difficulty of life."

1½ package **active dry yeast**

1 tbsp **sugar**

2 cups of warm **water** (105-110°F or 40-44°C)

1 tbsp **salt**

1 **egg white**

5 cups of the hardest, unbleached and highest rated protein white flour you can find.

Stoney-Buhr flour works well.

Mix the yeast, sugar and water in a large bowl. Then add the flour, adding more if needed for consistency. Turn the dough onto a floured surface and kneed it vigorously for about 10-12 minutes. Transfer the dough to a buttered bowl and turn it until the dough is totally coated with the butter. Cover the dough and let it rise in a warm, draft free place until it has doubled in size.

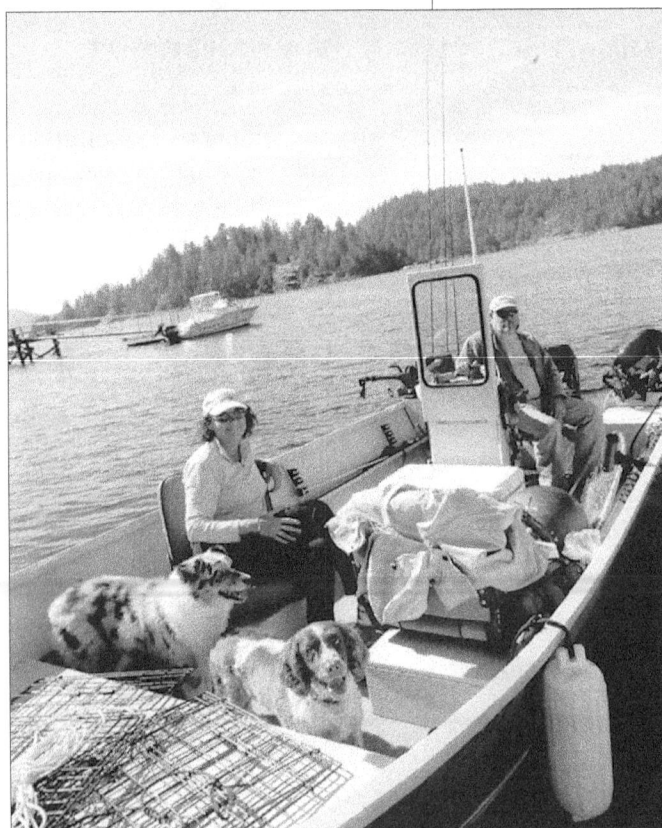

Then... push the dough down and divide it in half. Form each half into a long loaf, similar to the typical French Baguette and put them on a baking sheet that has been sprinkled with corn meal. Slash the top of the loaves diagonally in two or three places and then brush them with a mixture of one tablespoon water and one egg white.

Let the loaves rise for about 5 minutes and then put them in a cold oven, turning the temperature to 425° F or 220° C and bake the bread for 35-45 minutes or until it's crusty, brown and sounds hollow to a "tap". You can place a pan of boiling water under the loaves to make them crust and more "crunchy".

Eat the bread quickly as it goes stale in about 6 hours. You can freeze it after 2 hours if you want to save it for another occasion.

Cap Sparling

Whole Wheat Bread

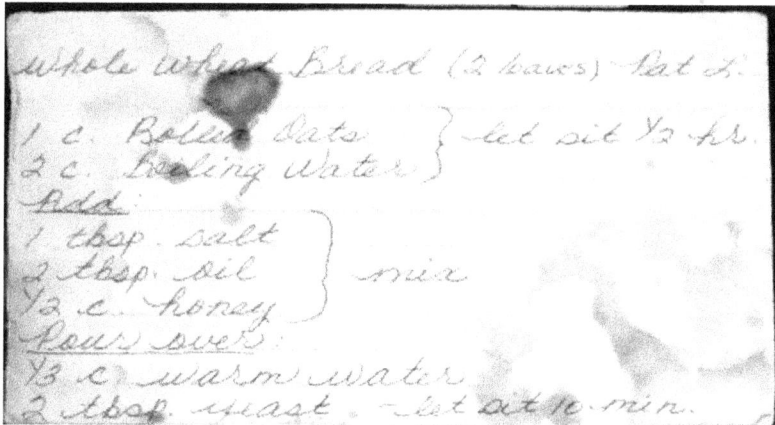

Whole Wheat Bread (2 loaves) - Pat L.

1 c. Rolled Oats   } let sit ½ hr.
2 c. boiling water }

Add:
1 tbsp. salt
2 tbsp. oil   } mix
⅓ c. honey
Pour over:
½ c. warm water
2 tbsp. yeast - let sit 10 min.

*Recipe written by Pat Lovell found
at the Hope House.*

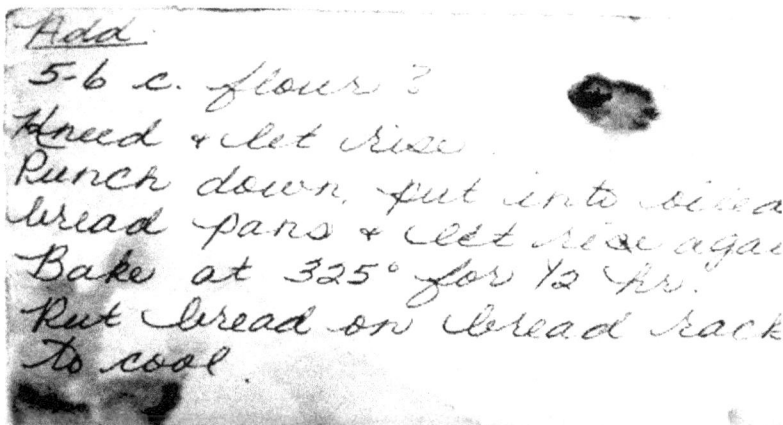

Add:
5-6 c. flour?
Knead & let rise
Punch down, put into bread
bread pans & let rise agai...
Bake at 325° for ½ hr.
Put bread on bread rack
to cool.

*Grains that are power packed
with nutrients are kasha,
quinoa, amaranth, barley and
oatmeal.*

*Buckwheat is wheat and
gluten free making it a great
alternative for those with
celiac disease and other wheat
allergies.*
*Grind up to make flour and
use instead of wheat.*

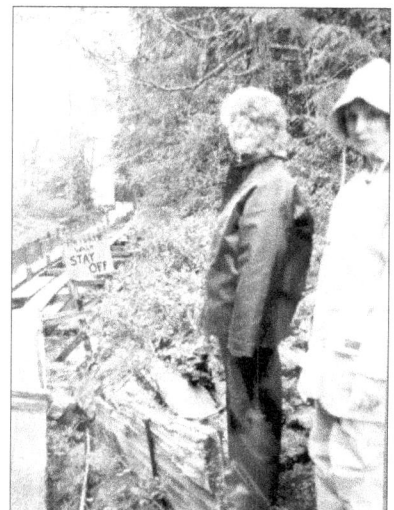

Pat and Dianna awaiting action at
flume at Refuge Cove. 1993

Photo by Lena Johnson

"Dorothy Thomas's dumpling recipe was found in a plastic bag of food related notes & clippings that were given to me by her daughter Betty Yexex when she was clearing out the house in the Hole.

They were written in a steno notebook dated 1961 when she was cooking at a logging camp in Ramsay Arm"

Judith Williams

Dumplings
2 cups Flour
1 tsp salt
½ tsp pepper
4 tsp Baking Powder
1 egg (beaten)
3 Tablespoons melted butter
about 2/3 cup milk

Sift dry ingr, add egg, butter & enough milk to make soft dough, drop into boiling liquid cover close, cook 15 min

Judy's Refuge Cove Story

The Store Party Dinner. Date 1978

The point of the party was for the store owners to fete the employees to celebrate surviving the summer tourist rush. I was to cook. It must be that this party was when Bobo and Don Woroeby were store owners and we still lived in the small house as I recall making the sauce there. The party was held at the Gibbons.

MENU

Cold spring salmon served with a "Sauce Provençale Pour Les Saumons" from Elizabeth David's *French Provincial Cooking*.

"La Daube De Boeuf Provençale"
(from the same cookbook)

Bobo French Bread

Watermelon Surprise.

A lot to drink.

I enlisted my neighbor Liz Magor to help and she arranged a long row of tables covered with sheets and then sewed a pristine row of Salal leaves down the middle. Everyone remembers this. We unscrewed a brass drawer handle from the armoire and she attached it to the top of the watermelon and amazed all by presenting a whole watermelon and lifting off the top with grace.

Sauce Provençale

Take a medium sized onion, 1 ½ oz. of capers and a substantial pinch of parsley.

Chop together after having washed the onion and parsley and wrung all dry in a cloth.

Take 3 or 4 rinsed anchovy fillets, 2 cooked yolks of eggs and 1 raw one.

Pound all together and incorporate, little by little, 8 fluid ounces of olive oil smelling of the fruit, and the juice of a lemon.

Salmon. Bake with salt and pepper & cool.

(continued on next page.)

Refuge Cove Store being renovated on the floating barge at the end of the boardwalk.

La Daube

David claims this is an easy recipe for 4-5 people. Ha! I think we had to specially order the pork rinds and I used ordinary smoked bacon.

  2 lb top rump of *beef*

  6 oz of *unsmoked bacon* or *salt pork*

  3 oz of *pork rinds*

  2 *carrots*

  2 *onions*

  2 *tomatoes*

  2 *garlic clove*

  a bouquet of *thyme, bay leaf, parsley* and a strip of *orange peel*

  2 tbsp *olive oil*

  a glass of *red wine* and

  seasoning

Cut the meat into postcard-sized pieces 1/3 inch thick and the bacon into cubes.

Peel and slice onions and carrots.

Cut pork rinds into small squares.

Skin and slice tomatoes.

In bottom of pot put olive oil, bacon, vegetables and half of the pork rinds. Arrange meat on top overlapping. Bury garlic cloves flattened, the bouquet in the center and the rest of the pork rinds on top. Heat up on the stove.

After ten minutes heat wine in another saucepan to a fast boil, set it alight and rotate pan so flames spread. When flames die down, pour wine over the meat pot.

(We did have a small fire extinguisher)

Cover pot with greaseproof paper or foil and a lid. Roast in oven for 2 ½ hours at 325°F.

At serving stage sprinkle over a persillade of finely chopped garlic and parsley with a few chopped anchovies and a few capers.

I more than tripled the recipe to feed 12 people and cooked it for 3 hours.

There was nothing left. There never was.

Watermelon

Cut off long oval from top.

Scoop out insides with melon baller. (I doubt we had one.)

Cut balls or cubes of cantaloupe add grapes, blueberries and strawberries.

Marinate in brandy with some sugar to taste.

Put all back in cleaned out watermelon just before dinner and refrigerate. I think....

We were pretty crazed by this time and it was a long, long time ago.

Judith Williams

Bobo's French Bread

Bobo & Judith's classic seiner Adriatic Sea, cruising along the coast.

You may be surprised to find me included in this volume, thinking me only a gifted consumer of food—but as you will see your surprise is without foundation. Every Christmas at Refuge Cove found me taking Julia Child volume 2 from the shelf, turning to page 57 and slavishly following the 20 odd page recipe to produce the best bread ever eaten in Canada. I have had bread that tasted as good and perhaps looked marginally better but that was at the finest restaurant in France near Bordeaux—it had 3 stars from Michelin then in 1978 and still does to this day.

If you want to cause a sensation not to mention fighting and recrimination among your friends and acquaintance just follow the recipe and set the result on a table. I don't believe much of my bread ever made it to Christmas dinner proper as competition to obtain more than a fair share led to astounding behavior from the entire Refuge Cove population, even the mildest and most self effacing of our membership. Think of a cross between a heavy metal mesh pit (whatever the fuck that is) and the Ultimate Fighting Championship and your imagining is not far off.

Bobo Fraser

The Refuge Years

Norm and Denise Gibbons

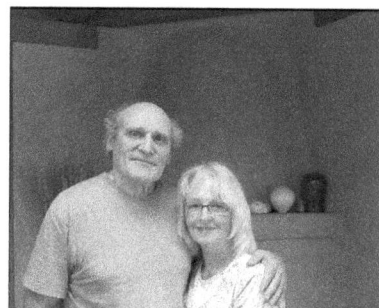

Thinking back over the Refuge years and the vast storehouse of memory, this one in particular seems as if it were yesterday. I had heard of this mythic place since I was 13 years old, when having just met Norm, he announced he was leaving Vancouver to go and work at Refuge Cove for the summer. No one I knew worked when they were 13 but that's another story. Every fall Norm would return with fantastic tales of this wonder land. Over the next 14 years I became good friends with Norman and Doris but always saw them in Vancouver where they would arrive for a town trip, but of course never together, as one always had to stay behind to mind the store. Uncle Norman would hold court at the Ritz Hotel, treating family and friends to many a wonderful meal there. Doris always stayed with Betty Gibbons and was always anxious for a bridge game during which she would regale us with her stories and anecdotes about every facet of life at the Cove. Not until I was 27 did I get to visit Refuge for the first time.

It was November, we arrived after dark, cold and tired and were welcomed into warmth and charm of Doris' parlour. In those days the oil furnace in the basement kept the whole house warm and cozy. Of course the TV was on, of course we drank Canadian Club rye (ugh) and of course we feasted on fish and chips. It was everything I had imagined. That night we slept in Norman's back bedroom, tucked under the old down duvet and fell asleep listening to the mesmerizing but astonishingly loud sound of the creek, coursing just a few feet below us. I swear that river of sound wove its magic through the night, rooting me to that land in a most powerful way.

Denise Gibbons

French Fried Rabbit

Skin, clean and wash rabbit thoroughly.

Cut into serving pieces.

Boil in salted water until tender (30 min.)

Drain water off.

Make a batter with 1/4 cup sifted flour, 1/2 tsp salt and 2 tbsp baking powder.

Beat together 2 eggs and 3 cups milk.

Mix thoroughly with dry ingredients.

Dip pieces of rabbit into batter coating well, then fry in pan with oil turning until golden brown.

Norm and Denise Gibbons have shared many stories about Refuge Cove. Norm, after many nights waiting to shoot the troublesome old bear, proudly succeeded and Denise continued to can and prepare bear in many imaginative ways. She even made bear lasagne. Nothing went to waste.

Soon after Reinhold shot and skinned a young bear and the discovered that bear didn't taste all that bad after all.

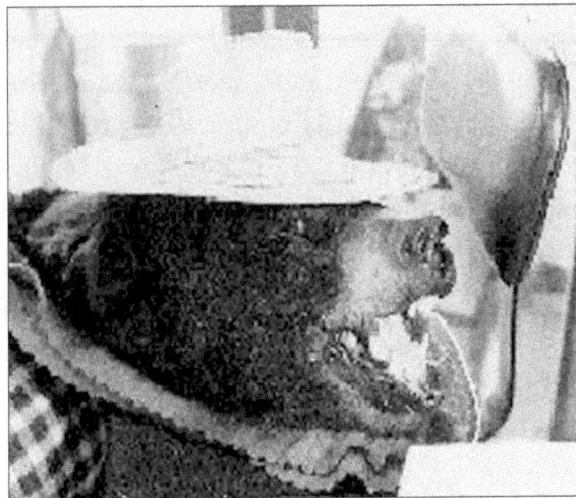

Bearskin.

Photo by Judy Williams

Bear grease was caught in clamshells while the bear cooked overhead.
It was used much like butter and mayonnaise are used today.

Bear BBQ-ed in chunks roasted over an open fire was a prized delicacy with the Coast Salish.

Some coastal women dried long bear meat muscles, separated strands into hanks of three and braided them for snacks.

It is very important to dress the bear out on the forest floor where it fell. Cut out the acorn gland in its knees, which make the good meat taste awful.

Meat from the bear is usually rich, tender and delicious, especially if the animal is under 3 years of age. Bears killed just before hibernation are fat from gorging on berries, roots and fish. The gamey flavour comes from the fat so it should be trimmed off before cooking. Bear should always be cooked until it is well done to kill any parasite that may be present.

Bear

"Norm and I dressed up as bunnies at the Refuge Cove Halloween party. In this image we are barbecuing the bear, forever known as the Bearbecue. Everyone but Norm had a stomach ache that night."

1981 Picture courtesy of Denise Gibbons

The noise was unexpected: a smashing sound from a scrub area to his right, a hundred yards distant, like a bulldozer had flared to life, a D-8 Cat at least. The beast racketed through salal, negotiated the forest without deviation. A straightforward demolition of the wilderness was underway: no conscience, no thought for stealth, brazen confidence. The noise rampaged by quickly and headed down to the other beehive site above Alice's house.

James took up his rifle.

The noise ceased. He calculated fifteen minutes passed and that was enough time for condensation on his gun barrel to turn into a thin film of ice. The noise started again but not nearly so bold. He guessed the bear behind him now, below him, somewhere near the base of the moss bluffs, had probably gone through his own yard. Another twig snapped – not a deer this time – then a crunch noise on scarcely frozen moss. He turned his head to look down on the bluff. The twisting cramped his leg. There was a new shape on the hillside, dark and round, motionless. The small moon was beginning to crest over a hill so the night was lighter than before. He couldn't remember a shape in that spot. His concentration created silence: no hum of the *L.O. Larson*, the jet had landed. No putt of Conner's' generator, no music from Jeremy's tape deck, no forest noise. Then the shape was on another ledge. James was twisted in his chair, trying to look back and down, his leg in agony, the bear higher on the bluff, closer and bigger, shapeless.

He cursed that he had left his sign on the moss. It was at the base of his fir tree, snuffling and panting, whiffing the piss, giving a dry cough; then it stood upright and clawed at the night.

James had determined earlier, that if by chance the bear came, he would wait until the animal was engrossed in the hives before turning on the light. The bear jumped down onto a flat outcrop where the "condos" were set – made a "woof" sound when he landed. James saw a lumbering blackness silhouetted against absolute blackness, and to the right of those images, the ghostly grayness of the beehives. It seemed the bear had satisfied himself, that all was well possibly, he thought, James had been and gone, or wasn't astute enough to conceive of danger high in the tree. The bear relaxed, anticipating the sweet honey, panting steadily, no longer attentive to caution, perhaps willing to discard one more life.

James pulled the butt of the rifle to his shoulder. The safety made a faint click. The bear didn't hear, or if it did, didn't care that a strange noise came from above. He took a deep breath and turned on the light. The bear had the lid off one hive and had removed two frames, taking the painstaking care of an experienced apiarist. The light didn't bother him. He didn't look up; in fact, he seemed grateful to finally to see what he was doing – maybe James was the moon.

"Where's the bear?" said Nicole, once he was back on the ground.

"Over the bluff."

Peter moved to the edge of the bluff; divots of moss were scattered here and there. He searched with his light.

"I don't see anything."

They inspected the ground for blood, bone fragments, tuffs of fur, pink and frothy lung tissue, but there was nothing. Disoriented bees crawled on the moss.

Jeremy said, "You said you got him."

"I said, I think I got him."

Heinrik said, "We all told you the scope would be useless."

"You also said he wouldn't come 'til after midnight." James was trying to shade his eyes from the lights.

They, one by one, cast their lights on the ground.

Then Heinrik asked, "What happened to the two-by-four?" And all lights went for the shot-up rung. James looked at the rung too, and then down at his left foot.

"Maybe I shot my foot."

They took turns helping him home. Conners was the most helpful. Whenever Nicole assisted, she gripped his wrist so hard it made the pain in his foot slip away. During the descent to his home, he was distracted by the stars. They had increased in intensity as if burnished by the crisp cold air. He wanted to comment on the spectacular sight, but felt embarrassed about mentioning such an unimportant thing. When near his house, James said he couldn't be sure if he hit the bear. He had doubts the bear had shown at all.

Peter, who had a first-aid ticket, got the boot off once they were inside the house. The bullet had grazed the fleshy side of James' foot above the small toe. His sock was soaked in blood. He fell asleep on the couch while Peter bandaged him. The children sat on the stairs to the loft. The people went home for the night and agreed to meet at daybreak and then they would search for the bear.

By Norm Gibbons

An excerpt from his now published book
"Sea Without Shores:
Book Two: Edge of Desolation Trilogy"

Dec. 22/86
1 Deer.
Canned —

Salted — 2 Shoulders — Jan 14
3 weeks   1 loin

Pickled — brisket
              (do 9 days)

Venison

Corned Venison

6 qts. water	Combine all ingredients
2 cups pickling salt	but meat in large pot.
1/2 cup brown sugar	Bring to boil.
2 tbsp. pickling spice	When cold, add meat
1 tbsp. whole cloves	& stir around.
1 tbsp. peppercorns	Leave 2-3 weeks. Stir
2 bay leaves	every few days or so.
2 tbsp. salt peter - optional	Rinse well, boil or
6 cloves garlic	can.

Pat's Corned Deer Recipe

Bobo and Judy exploring. Year 2000

Venison

In 1986, I had my first sabbatical from UBC and Bobo and I moved to the new log house at Refuge for the year. Paul offered us part of a skinned and gutted deer. Bobo was to dismember it and I to preserve it. Now we did not have any power in the winter, no fridge or freezer so Pat wrote out instructions about canning, salting and pickling. I borrowed Reinhold's canner and canned a fair bit. I salted down the shoulders as per instructions. We ate the rest as fast as we could and in as many ways as I could invent. I picked wild mushrooms and juniper berries.

Then John Dixon came by with a small deer. I was having homesteading fatigue at this point and I was supposed to be working on a group of paintings as the point of my sabbatical, so Bobo skinned the deer as best he could; hung it up in the shed and we hacked off parts as needed. I painted. It was cold.

One day I went out and found two Stellar jays sitting on the carcass and they'd eaten a baseball-sized hole in the best part of the haunch. We enclosed the beast within a tarp but the birds were back the next day with a friend plotting a break and enter. At the end of the two deer I announced I would not cook any more deer for a while. Now I miss it.

Judith Williams

Judy salting down the deer.
Photo from Liz Magor

Deer Bourguignon

Cut up 4 pounds of **deer** into bite size pieces.

Place in a bowl covered with **Burgundy wine** and chopped **garlic** and let marinade overnight.

Strain meat and dredge with **flour** then season with **salt** and **pepper**.

Heat 2 tbsp **olive oil** and 1 tbsp **butter** in a heavy pot and brown the meat on all sides.

Remove the meat.

Brown 2 tbsp **flour** in the pot then add 1 cup of **broth** and one cup of **wine** which was drained from the meat and blend well. Add a **bay leaf** and a couple tablespoons **tomato paste**.

Return the meat to the pot cover and simmer slowly for 2 hours. Add the 2 chopped **carrots**, 4 small **onions**, 1 **green pepper** chopped, and 8 **mushrooms** and simmer until the vegetables are tender.

Serve with boiled potatoes.

Matt & Alister at Upcoast
Summer Restaurant. 2011

Refuge Cove Stew

The diet of squirrel consists mainly of nuts and berries. The flesh is medium red, is tender and has a truly delicious flavour. Be sure to remove the waxy scent glands inside the forelegs, wash thoroughly and remove all loose hair.

Cut into serving pieces 3 squirrel. Place in a large kettle with 3 quarts water. Bring to a slow boil reduce heat and simmer for 2 hours or until meat is tender, skimming surface occasionally. Remove meat from bone and return to liquid.

Add chopped bacon, ¼ tsp cayenne, 1 tsp sugar, 2 tsp salt, ¼ tsp pepper, 1 cup chopped onion, 2 cups canned tomatoes, 2 cups diced potatoes and 2 cups lima beans fresh or frozen.

Cook another hour. Add 2 cups corn and cook 10 minutes. Transfer to a buttered casserole dish. Top with 1/2 cup bread crumbs mixed with 2 tbsp melted butter.

Bake for 20 minutes at 375°F until crumbs are golden brown.

Serves 6

Venison Shish Kabob

Venison defrosted in fridge and aged (sealed well from air) for several days to a week.

Cut venison into large cubes (approx 1 1/2 inch squared) removing muscle lining and connective tissue as you go.

Marinade in equal parts chili/garlic paste (Red Rooster brand but in the jar) and Soy sauce. Use a lot!

Add fresh diced garlic. Add canola oil. Cover and marinade for 24 hrs, stirring a few times. Feel free to marinade your onions and peppers with the meat.

Don't do that to your mushrooms dummy...

Also don't forget to soak your skewers.

Cook over high heat on BBQ, and do not serve more cooked than medium rare.

Matt Dixon

Venison Stock

Shoot the deer. Skin the deer. Bring your deer home by boat. Bone out all the neck and front shoulders. Make hamburger meat out of that. Use the hind legs for the roasts.

Bone out all the venison.

Throw all the goodies, the marrow, meat and bones into a large stewing pot.

Chop up cabbage, two chopped up onions, chopped celery.

Add to pot of boiling bones.

Reduce it to a demi glaze cooking on a wood stove for three days.

Leave the lid off the pot as it cooks down..

Put the stock through a colander removing all bones and solids.

Put stock into sterilized quart canning jars. Put jars in a pressure cooker for 1/2 hour at 10–15 lbs.

This will make a very rich broth for soups and gravy.

Don Wicks

Don Wicks "Butcher"

Shoot the deer.

Skin the deer.

Bring your deer home by boat.

Bone out all the neck and front shoulders.

Make hamburger meat out of that.

Take out the back bone.

Use the hind legs for the roasts.

Deer gets dressed out.

Hang it.

Wild Thing.
The Night of the
Dancing Salami

Our acquaintance with the marten began on what our family calls The Night of the Dancing Salami, but it was actually more twilight than dark when Matthew and I came back to the Barnes Bay house from a December afternoon of fishing.

As we came through the French doors off the porch, there was enough Desolation Sound sunset left that we didn't have to stumble around for matches. There was a comforting sizzle and hiss from the kettles on top of the wood stove, and I threw in some more old-growth fir bark as Matthew lit our propane lamp. Our big Lab puppy, Cavall, snuffled around his food dish a bit and then became interested in something over by the fridge and bath tub.

Now I realize that I should pause here and explain the odd conjunction of bathroom and kitchen appliances in this house, but it would take too long to do justice to the topic. It's all about the difficulties of building things without power tools in the wilderness and the totally unreasonable domestic standards of my wife, Sandie.

Sandie imagines that an actual bathroom already exists, just outside the wall by the fridge, though we are temporarily frustrated by my wicked refusal to remove one or two trivial obstacles to its enjoyment, such as actually building it.

So she got out her hand-drills and saws one day and installed the bath tub herself, to provide all of us with the delights of candle-lit baths, and me in particular with a standing reproach.

Anyway, the tub sits right there by the fridge. Cavall was heading toward it and slowly coming up into the serious sort of point he reserves for grouse. There was an odd sound coming from the space between the tap end of the tub and the large bar that the kitchen sink lives in; a rustling and – but this could not be – muffled grunts, moans, and hisses. The light from the propane lamp was too far away to really help much, but from five feet it looked as though something fairly big was swaying back and forth on the floor. Matt grabbed a flashlight from the kitchen table, and it's light pushed us right through Alice's hole in the garden wall.

It was a very large dancing salami. The very salami, in fact, that I had brought for the Christmas season – a full and glorious two foot long Genoa wonder. It was standing upright on the floor, gyrating, swaying and making sounds that I have not heard accompany dancing since I used to hang out at the Steppenwolf bar in 1960's Berkeley. This was one horny, turned on, freaked out salami, and it looked to be getting ready to do the wild thing on our kitchen floor.

Matthew and I locked onto point with the dog, and we held those poses like field champions as the salami suddenly stood stock still and silent for about five seconds. Then three things happened almost instantaneously: the salami fell flat on the floor, a big pine marten shoved his head up the old drain hole (Sandie's first effort was off by about 8 inches) for the bath tub, and the dog levitated a minimum of six feet (Matthew insists eight, but he is not a reliable witness) straight backward to resume his point closer to the safety of the door.

Now this is the sort of moment, when the knitting starts to work on a torn Gestalt, that you expect to feel a kind of psychic relief. The marten had been trying to pull a plus 3" thick salami down a minus 3" hole, and was going nuts with frustration. The salami wasn't really alive, and the marten was making all of the noise. What seemed real was, after all, only apparent; the universe was restored to ordinary function; we were sane again. But all of these possible comforting thoughts were now completely displaced by the wonder of the marten himself. How could such a big head come through such a little hole – his seemed to be about the size and shape of a fox, but in chocolate brown with beautifully edited ears – and what sort of animal looked at people like this!?

Actually, his quick eyes had taken in the dog first, and with one fierce glance he sent a transmission out to Cavall in animal Esperanto: "just take one step you big #$%&!!@ dummy, and you'll be carrying that stupid black nose of yours around in a baggy." That accomplished,

he turned his attention to Matthew and I, and I have never been fixed, by any animal other than a 200 pound timber wolf, with such a glare of utterly calm, self-possessed disdain.

Stupidly – almost as though I couldn't wait to confirm his prejudices – I yelled at him...."Yowwwie!" His worst judgment of us now confirmed, he waited just long enough to prevent any possibility of misinterpreting his movement as flight, and then made a dignified withdrawal down the drain hole. A couple of noises from the sub-floor and he dropped onto the ground. Gone.

"Wow!" Matt said, "that was beautiful. What was it?" "A pine marten", I explained, "the largest member of the weasel family unless you count in wolverines." Which was not, of course, an explanation, but just some sounds to pass the time with why we were both recovering from what was, in truth, an apparition and miracle. Because sometimes the world can get in behind the language of understanding, utterly eluding even our most subtle and comprehensive systems of bookmarks. Then it can reveal itself in an instant – even between the everydayness of bath tub and refrigerator – as pure, wild wonder.

John Dixon, 1993

"The pigs up the hill often got loose. One time the whole group of piglets got loose and the tide was coming in. Judy was afraid they were dumb enough they might drown.

To catch the pigs Judy mixed porridge with home brew and put it into pails while chowing down the front legs of the pigs fell into the pail. They were getting sloshed in the process. They would eat while she dragged the pail backward up the steep incline to their pen in the forest."

Judith Williams

How to skin a pig

Place in boiling hot water. The problem was they just couldn't keep the water hot enough!

N. Gibbons

Head - Cheese

½ Pigs-Head,2 small pigs-feet,
2 lbs veal or beef tongue, 1 onion,
3 table spoon salt,water to cover all,
boil till meat falls off the bones,
chop up meat,add 3table-spoon nutmeg,
1 table-spoon pepper,about 1½ qts of
juice, mix-well,add ¼ cup vinegar mix,

put in pans, let cool before refrigeratio

Pathe De Foie Gras

Leaf-Lard,is from the inside of the pigs
you should have some,if you have,use it,
it is much better.

3½ lbs pork fat,(1)onion grind-to-gether
3 lbs pork-liver,(2)tea-spoon salt-peter
grind,pork-fat,liver,salt-peter (to-gether)

add- (1)table-spoon salt,(1)T.sp-pepper
     (1)table-spoon mace,mix-mix-mix,

     Line pan'ssliced 1/8 ins.back-fat
     sides & bottom,seal with your-finger
     you should have Approx 7-81bs.meat.

     Fill your pan's ¼ ins from top.
     Cook for 4½ hrs in a (225 oven

Recipe from Brenda and Bill Finch from Portage Cove. Brenda must have canned a lot of bear and deer. Their closest neighbours were on a game trail. They sold vegetables to the store.

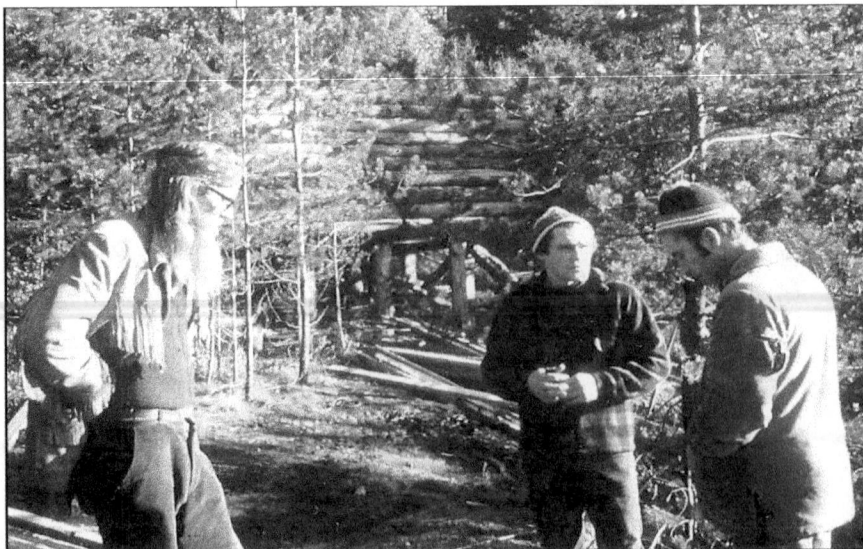

Peter Kyte, Norm & Barry building the log house.

Courtesy of Judith Williams

Hoge's Fast Foods

Breakfast at 7 am to 10 am. *Eggs, back bacon & cheese on an English muffin & coffee or tea for breakfast. Sometimes Hanne made cinnamon buns.*

Lunch 11 am to 2 pm sharp. *Hamburgers & Home Fries.*

No substitutes!

Barbara Emry helped him in the kitchen.

Early 1980's new building for Hoge's Fast Foods. Below – Hoge, Hanne, Donna, Dave & Les.

Pictures courtesy of Frieda Home

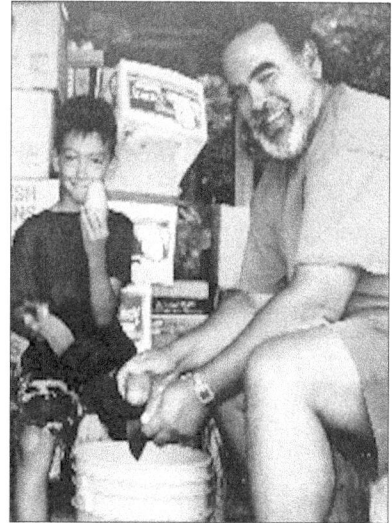

"Early every morning John & Alden and whoever else volunteered for a free breakfast, would faithfully go scrub russet potatoes with a pot scrubber and a pail of cold water for Reinhold's famous home fries. They would then peel them. Now you had to do this the right way or you were fired. I was canned at least twice and I think John was fired too. No breakfast for us!"

Cathy Campbell

S ounds of Desolation Sound: hearing the eagles wings soar, the ravens song, prehistoric call of the heron, hawks high pitched screech, hummingbirds dive-bombing wing whistle, wolves howling at the moon, seals splashing to gather food or warn their young, whales blowing, water lapping, trees swooshing in the wind, a nighthawk's sonic swooping as it feeds, thrush and songbirds evening serenade.....tides breathing with us the vitality of the life force. Laughter and joy and The sound of silence.

Sights – Snow capped, mist rolling over the mountains, the many subtle shades of green of flora and fauna, mercury ocean, spectacular black velvet sunsets. Reflections. Happy smiles.

Smells – Ocean, seaweed, fish and oysters, forest cedar, spruce, pine resin, honey beeswax, fresh clean air and otter.

Feel – liquid gold sunshine, warm summer saltwater , gentle breeze kisses and a constant humming song of joy in my heart and gratitude for being here.

Taste of Desolation – all of the above plus the friends and harvests from the ocean and land all around us.

Rum Ribs

4 lbs **pork ribs**

1 cup **brown sugar**

½ cup **chili sauce**

¼ cup **ketchup**

½ cup or more **dark rum**

¼ cup **Worcestershire sauce**

2 **garlic** cloves, crushed

¼ tsp **pepper**

Wrap ribs in double thickness of foil. Bake in roasting pan at 350°F for 1 ½ hour. Unwrap and drain.

Combine all ingredients and pour over ribs.

Marinate at room temperature for 2 hours.

Broil or barbeque, turning and basting often.

Francie Hill

Oriental Meatballs

Colin made this dish. It was a family Christmas favourite.

2 slices **bread**

1 lb **ground beef** *or* **venison**

1 **egg**

1 tsp **salt**

1 tsp powdered **ginger**

½ tsp powdered **garlic**

3 tbsp **corn starc**h

1 tbsp **vegetable oil**

½ cup **sugar**

¼ cup **soy sauce**

½ cup **vinegar**

½ cup **dry sherry**

Moisten bread with water and squeeze dry. Combine salt, meat and eggs, mustard, garlic powder and ginger. Blend well.

Form in 1" balls. Roll in cornstarch then brown in oil. Drain off excess fat. Combine sugar, vinegar, soy sauce and wine. Pour over meatballs. Simmer, basting occasionally until sauce thickens and meat balls are glazed.

Colin Robertson

Colin recalls the old days at Refuge Cove Store when, in the corner of the store where the cash register now is, was Rob's Deli.
Colin had never seen such efficient tidiness.

Rob made great pies – rabbit, hamburger, beef & quiche. Colin also has very fond memories of Reinhold's mothers delicious schwenkbraten schnitzel. He always wondered if she had made it the day the cougar paid a visit to Reinhold's home.

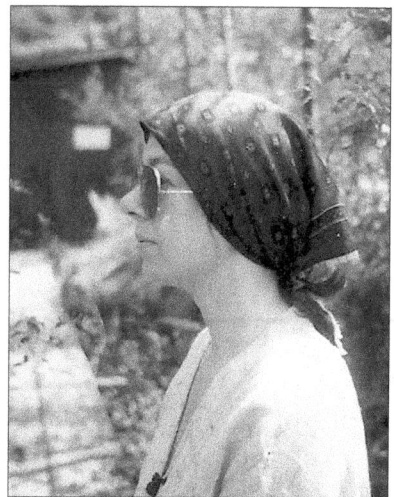

Bonnie MacDonald.

Photo courtesy of Judith Williams

Corrine and her loyal dog Spencer.

Green Meatloaf

$\mathcal{S}$et oven to 350° F

Combine:

onions chopped and sautéed

1 lb **ground meat**

1 **egg**

parsley

bread crumbs

lemon juice (1 tsp)

salt & pepper

Optionally, also add:

grated **carrot**, ¼ **apple** grated, **lemon** peel, **oats** instead of bread crumbs

Combine about 8 oz **feta, herbs: basil, oregano, garlic powder, dried tomato, etc.**

Cook and drain a big bunch of **spinach.**

Place ½ meat mixture in a greased oven pan.

Cover with feta mixture as second layer.

Cover with spinach.

Finally use all of the other ½ meat mixture as final layer.

Bake 1 hour.

Although this recipe only has one egg in it, I get that egg from my chickens here at Refuge.

Corrine Corry

Delia, Mary & Spencer helping Corrine bring her first chickens to Refuge. July 2009.

Photo by Corrine Corry

Liver Pate

Fry up bacon and onion.

Toss in locally sourced livers sautéed with bacon and onion.

Season with smoked paprika.

Add a dash of brandy or port to flavour.

If you haven't eaten this dish up already.

Cool then puree in food processer.

Do not eat the liver of bear as it is excessively high in Vitamin A, so much so that it is very toxic to humans.

Pelton Wheel designed and build by Don Wicks.

The schwenker allows grilling over an open fire even when there are flames. Varying height and amount of swinging allows for fine tuning of heat of meat.

The pork cutlets should be marbled to ensure juiciness. Grill slowly about 20 minutes to the point where the upside starts beading moisture than turn only once at this point to cook until done (about 5 minutes.)

Schwenkbraten (from "Das Kochbuch aus dem Saarland" 1977)

Ingredients:
per person one thick boned neck pork cutlet (butt)
spice marinade per 10 cutlets:
salt, pepper, 1 tbsp crushed thyme, 1tbsp oregano, 4 cloves garlic, a few crushed bay leaves, 1 tsp clove powder, 15 crushed juniper berries, 1 tsp allspice powder, obstler (clear, non-sugared fruit brandy))

Instructions: Rub meat with salt. Mix remaining spices in small bowl. In a wide bowl alternate layers of onions, spice mixture, and meat finishing with a layer of onions. Let rest 12-24 hours. When putting on grill ("schwenker") remove all onions. Grill about 1/2 hour depending on thickness of meat. The "obstler" is for the cook and lookers-on during the "schwenking". This meal is usually accompanied with ample white bread (french type) and beer. As an elegant alternative, serve with a selection of salads & a hearty red wine.

Schwenkbraten written by Reinhold. 1977

Reinhold at "schwenker," grilling the meat.
Photo Courtesy of Frieda Home

RIB B-B-QUE

First you must find a 60 inch in diameter grill that swings over an open pit. Thanks to Reinhold and Barry that problem was already resolved.

Second purchase enough racks of pork ribs to feed 35 to 50 of your closest friends. The day prior to the event defrost the ribs and steam them for 20 to 30 minutes each. After each rack has been steamed a dry rub of Mexican spices, cayenne pepper and garlic powder is hand applied to the still hot ribs. (Make sure you are careful not to get stung by all the wasps this process attracts.)

The ribs are then placed in a very large cooler full of block ice. The afternoon of the party a barbeque sauce is prepared. Combine one quart of ketchup, one cup of honey, the juice of 4 lemons, 3 oz. extra hot horse radish, 2 tbsp. dry mustard, 3 oz. Worcestershire sauce and just enough Tabasco to suit the tastes of your guests.

Start the charcoal one hour prior to the arrival of your first guests. Arrange the hot coals around the outside edge of the pit banked about 4 inches high. The center of the pit doesn't need any coals as this area of the grill will serve as a location to rest the ribs as the cooking continues. 40 pounds of charcoal is enough to cook that much meat.

Begin grilling the ribs as the first guests begin arriving. Using a 4 inch paintbrush (unused previously) apply a generous portion of sauce to both sides of the ribs which have now been cut into 4 or 5 sections for easy handling. Continue to turn and baste the ribs until lightly charred. Now it's time to have another drink and enjoy the party!

Sinker and Frieda
grilling ribs at the gazebo.

"Norman Hope taught me how to cut up the meat. I became the butcher in the store.

People would cruise on their boats into the cove every day for their choice cuts of fresh meat and fish.

Monty, who believed in living off the earth's bounty would hunt and at times there would be a raccoon or skinned squirrel hanging in the freezer at the store.

Everything changed after the oil embargo tripled in price.

Fewer and fewer boats came in to the docks."

Norm Gibbons

Tamale Casserole (Carol)
1½ lb. ground round   14 oz can tomatoes
½ C. chopped onion   13 oz kernel corn
½ C   pepper   4 oz black olives
1 tsp sea. 1 cl. garlic minced · Corn meal topping
Hot spices   Grated cheddar
· Brown meat, add on   · salt, spices
· tomat. Simmer 10 mins.· Add corn
olives. mix well Spread in dish

Great recipe from Carol Emmons Circa 1972.

Courtesy of Denise Gibbons collection

Topping
2 eggs
1 C. milk well beaten
1 C. corn meal
  (baking powder) - Spread mixt.
on top. Bake 40-50 mins.
Sprinkle cheese on top, bake
another 5 mins.
                    350°

Mel and Greg at the dock with Widget. 1978

Photo from Lena Johnson Jan. 1978

Oven Baked BBQ Ribs

Famous ribs using a can of Coke.

    1 can of **Coke**

    3 cloves of **garlic**

    3/4 cup of **brown sugar**

    1/2 cup **soy sauce**

    2 tbsps. **cornstarch**

    2 tbsps. **vinegar**

Place all above ingredients in a saucepan and cook until sauce thickens. Place ribs in a 9 x 13 pan and pour sauce over ribs.

Place in 300° oven and cook for 2-1/2 to 3 hours. Baste with sauce every hour or so. Will work for up to at least four racks of ribs.

Be sure to turn half-way through cooking.

Jim Lusse

Sharon & Jim Lusse in their boats and Sharon in her coastal kitchen.

GLoP

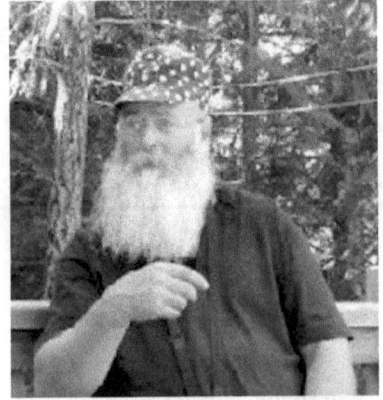

Ground **moose meat** and diced **onions** cooked up in a large cast iron frying pan

Boil **macaroni** drain

Add to moose mixture.

Add can of **tomatoes**

Season with **chili powder**

When Fraser came over for breakfast I would make him eggs, fried bread and fried bologna.

Mel Hart

"In those days people canned salmon, bear, venison and butter clams. There was a lot of clamming at Dorothy's lease. Corrine and Judy often dug up horse clams in front of Pat & Paul's place."

Recollection in 1974

Star fishing for the garden.

Photo by Lena Johnson

Frieda, Bradley and fresh venison sausages hanging above.

"We were a part of the community from the start of the cooperative, 1972 to about 1985.

Albert was very involved and interested in the idea. I remember one summer when I decided to earn some extra money by selling some food in the store. Albert got a commercial fishing license & we smoked some cod to sell. I also baked pies. They sold so well, the Cove residents were buying them up so fast the tourists didn't have a chance.

I also worked in the store in the evenings during the summer for a couple of years. It was interesting to see how often the members came there to see what they could put together for dinner.

Albert remembers that we had a log moving and wall raising events to help one another building homes. He knew that there would be a good bowl of chili and beer after the job was done."

Anne and Albert Melul

Photographs courtesy of Frieda Home

43

Prune Stuffed Goose

Excellent Dish   Done perfectly Christmas 75
                                              Refrig Corn
Prune Stuffing for Goose   on oven heated
                                   oil stove

40 prunes (pitted)
   soak 5 mins in hot water ✓
      pit
2/3 cup Vermouth
2 cup stock
   Simmer prunes etc - 10 mins
      drain & reserve stock

   Goose liver
   Shallots | Sauté 2 mins ✓
   Butter

Scrape into bowl ✓

2/3 Cups of Vermouth
   Boil wine in Skillet till ⅓ left ✓
      Add to liver   make liver paste by cooking

Blend liver paste into Goose liver livers
      - need 4 oz ✓
   If too soft Add 2T bread stuffing

Fill prune with Stuffing
Stuff loosely goose
Prick skin & dry

15 mins in hot oven
lower to (350°) - turn Goose on side
                   turn other side & on back
10-12 lbs   2 hrs. 20 mins   15 mins before end

Spoon out fat
   - Add prune juice & ⅓ cup port
   - boil it down - Swirl in butter

Set goose on platter & surround with parsley
Pass sauce in Sauce boat

Refuge Cove Christmas Dinner

Bobo had undertaken the making of his French bread for the 1975 Refuge Cove Xmas dinner at Hope House. Bud, who was living at Tiber Bay, had a goose and I decided to cook it as part of the dinner. I remember so many people turned up from the surrounding area you could not move thru the Hope's house once you got in and that may account for the shockingly un-cooperative behavior of certain people.

I based my recipe on a version of a Julia Child pate' stuffed goose served to me by a Vancouver friend. At that time, Bobo and I lived in a 12x12 cottage while we finished the big log house and getting the culinary materials and equipment assembled in the house was challenging. The wood fired oven was small. However, the goose was stuffed and roasted, it and the bread transported to Hope's house and stashed in the back bedroom. A couple of turkeys were being rowed from other directions and a variety of vegetables and condiments jostled for position on the kitchen table.

A couple of glasses of wine emboldened Bobo to brag about the excellence of both his bread and the goose. He led Bud, Norm, Denise and I to the back bedroom to inspect the big bird. It seemed evident that a small taste was essential to ascertain just how successfully it had been cooked. The skin was a masterpiece of crispy deliciousness. The hours of basting with boiling water had not been in vain. We took sample of the breast and another of the leg. We nibbled a wing. Those samples were also good. In fact they were excellent. They were the best thing we'd eaten in recent memory. We may have ripped off hunks of bread to soak up the juices. Possibly we shut the door.

I don't really recall who was carving but in the blink of an eye the goose was gone. We stared at the carcass and then silently joined the forty-odd people in the rest of the house. We never mentioned the goose.

Judith Williams

Photo: Bobo, Judy and Bud, Xmas dinner. 1975

Courtesy of Judith Williams

Bonnie and Bernie

Refuge Cove Chicken Curry

4 frozen **chicken thighs** with skin (this is not for weight watchers)

1 large **onion**

4 **peaches** or **nectarines** depending on what is on the self in the back of the store

1 can **coconut milk**

2 tbsp **curry powder** this is not fancy, we're basically camping

1 tbsp **grated ginger** or 1 tsp powder

For four people (just keep expanding if you end up with 10 people!)

Fry defrosted chicken slowly until skin is brown and lots of chicken fat is in the pan. Take out chicken and add diced onion to the fat in the pan. Fry onion slowly until brown but not burnt. Fry grated ginger for a minute or two. Add curry powder and fry for a minute until it's toasted. Do not burn or you will have to through the whole lot out and start again). Add diced peaches or nectarines (without skins). Fry for a couple of minutes. Then add coconut milk and chicken to the pan. Simmer for 1 hour, add water if it gets too thick. Serve over rice (*Basmati is the best*)

This recipe is wonderful for prawns also.

Bernie Hughes

One winter we got Bobo to go buy a turkey for a big Christmas dinner at Auntie Doris's place. He came back with the biggest turkey he could find. It must have weighed at least 38 pounds.

Norm Gibbons and Don set it up on the butcher block in the store and Don, who was fresh out of cooking school, deboned it starting with the backbone. He cut out the carcass and sewed it up again with butcher thread. They stuffed it with dressing and it came out at 40 lbs. They threw it in the propane oven and it roasted for twelve hours, from 6 am until 6 pm.

They started up the generator and got out the electric knife to slice it up for serving.

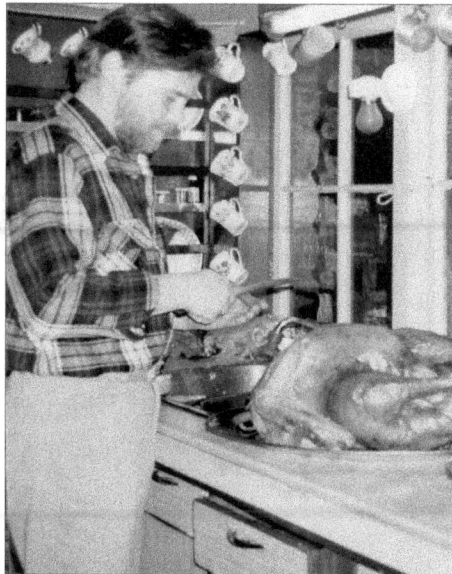

Don carving the Christmas turkey at the Hope's cabin.

Photo courtesy of Don Wicks

Hasenpfeffer

1 small **rabbit**, cleaned and cut into serving pieces (2 1/4 pounds)
½ cup **vinegar**
2 cups **water**
2 tsp **salt**
¼ tsp **pepper**
2 tsp whole **cloves**
2 tsp **sugar**
4 bay **leaves**
1 sliced **onion**
2 tsp **Worcestershire sauce**
3 tbsp **flour**
3 tbsp **fat**

Make pickling mix in a bowl. Add rabbit and giblets and cover bowl. Marinate in refrigerator 12 hours or so turning to absorb marinade evenly. Remove rabbit. Discard bay leaves. Save marinade.

Roll rabbit in flour. Heat a skillet and brown rabbit on all sides. Pour marinade into pan with rabbit. Cover and cook on low heat 1 hour or so. Remove rabbit from pan. Add Worcester sauce with a little water.

Thicken with flour stirring until smooth gravy forms. Pour over rabbit.

"When Aunt Doris invited fishermen for dinner she made them take off their clothes and take a shower before they ate. They would take turns using Uncle Normans dressing gown. They often got their clothes washed. The washer, dryer and shower were in the store, so they had to walk down the boardwalk with the dressing gown on."

Joan Carter

Don Wicks, in the early 1970's.
He was a commercial salmon fisherman.

Photo courtesy of Don Wicks

Summer of salmon. 2011

Fishing in Desolation Sound; resident winter Chinook are not as large as the spring and summer runs of Chinook and Coho. Chum runs through in the fall. Pinks may be caught in August but are not very common. There are no Sockeye in this area. If the Orca are coming through don't expect to catch anything!

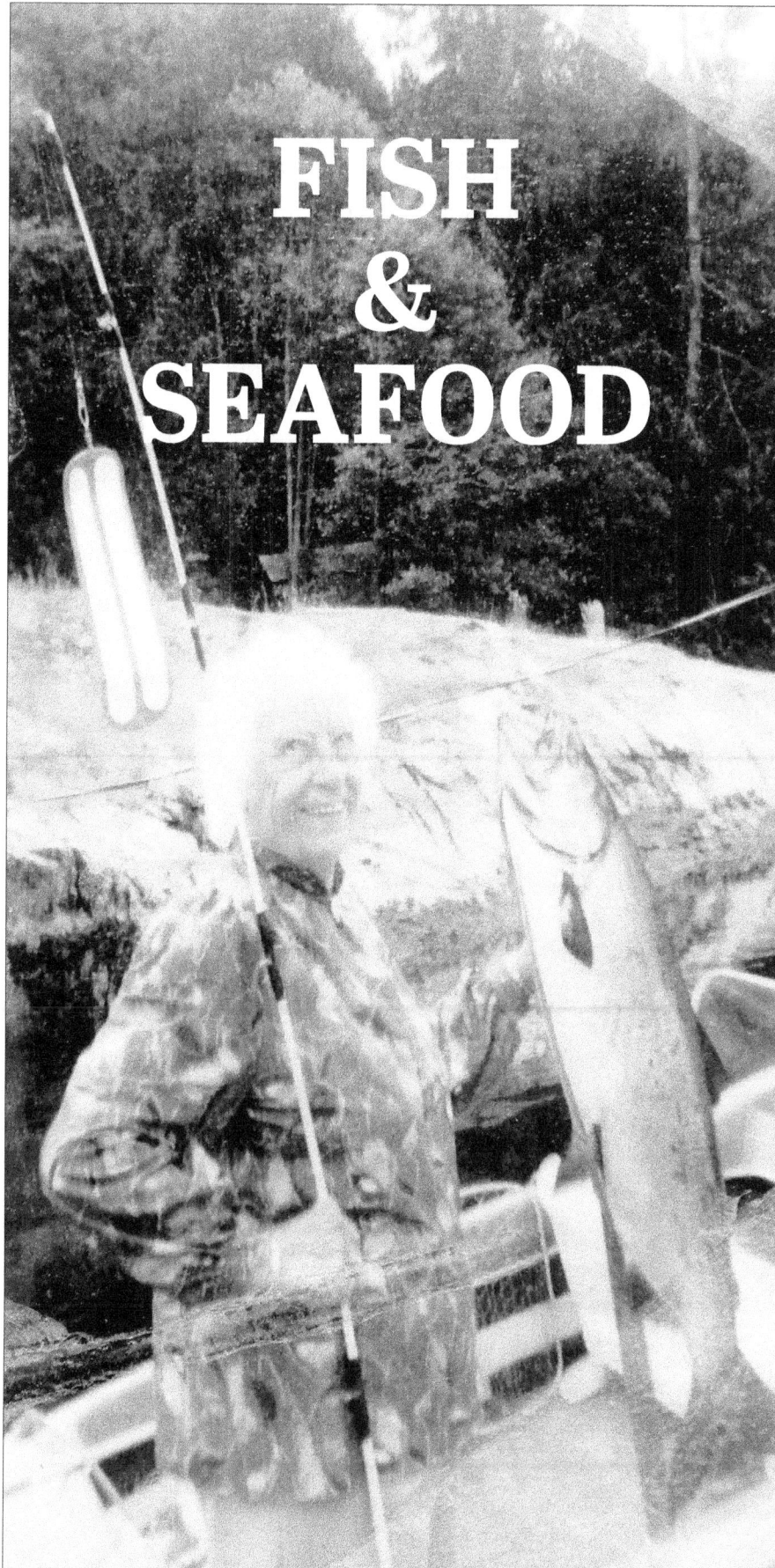

FISH
&
SEAFOOD

"The residents of Refuge Cove have fond recollections of going over to Doris Hope's cabin for cod fry and chips. She had the deep fryer set up on the back porch outside of the kitchen. She would get that fryer going and cook them up countless deep fried cod and chips. She would holler out, just keep ordering you fuckers!"

Don Wicks

49

Cranberry Salsa

1 cup dried **cranberries**

1 20-ounce can **pineapple** tidbits, reserving 1/4 cup juice

1/4 cup chopped **red pepper**

1/4 cup chopped fresh **cilantro**

2 tablespoons chopped **red onion**

1 tablespoon **jalapeno pepper**, seeded and minced

2 teaspoons **lime** peel, freshly grated

1/4 teaspoon salt

Combine all ingredients in large bowl and mix well.

Cover and refrigerate for 2 hours to allow flavors to blend.

Serve with fish, poultry or meat.

"Desolation Sound Salmon Enhancement Society Refuge Cove B.C." Signs constructed and designed courtesy of Reinhold Hoge

Salmon R Us

*S*cott Rempel and Delia Becker. The salmon people. The heart, soul, muscle, and sinew of salmon enhancement efforts in Desolation Sound.

And the brains. Trained as biologists, they have brought a scientific background to the work, and the intellectual discipline needed to braid together the loose strands of fact, hypothesis, and wild supposition that comprise what little we know/believe about the life histories of the wonderful fish whose voluntary musculature we love to eat.

And stamina. Bringing back the salmon isn't a job for flighty enthusiasts; it's a long haul work-of-generations thing, and Scot and Delia have anchored the sometime contributions of the rest of us by never taking their shoulders from the wheel. Thanks be that Delia and Scott have become such an integral part of our community. Long may it be so.

John Dixon

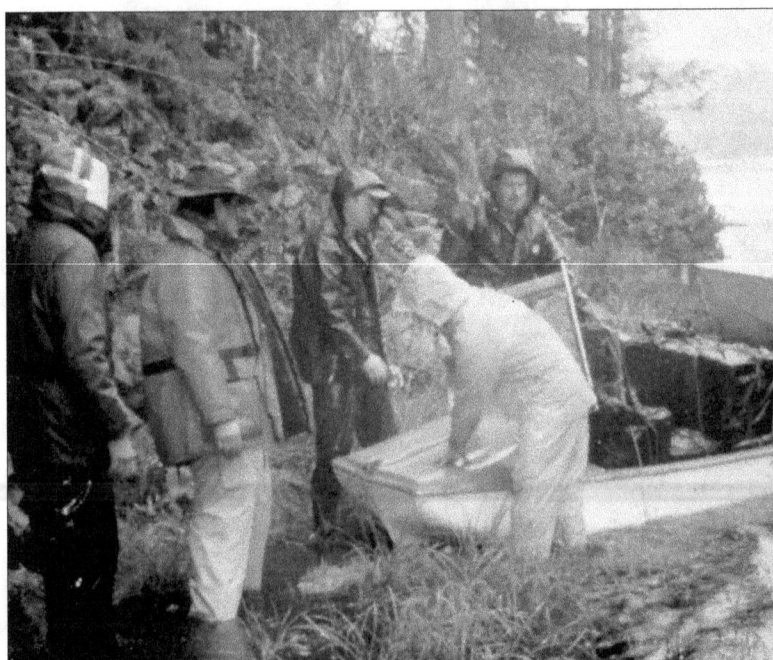

Delivering salmon fry one rainy winter day up the lagoon to Jeep Creek. 1996.

Kieran
Jarvis &
Rick Carter

**Photo
courtesy
of Jackie
Frioud.**

Gazebo Party
Potluck and fish fry
gathering.

Reinhold planned to host a fish fry every two weeks when the deep fryer oil was to be replaced for fresh oil for the fries at the hamburger stand.

In the beginning people would catch fish, then a friend of Doris supplied lingcod.

When the daily catch was limited to one lingcod this put an end to the regular fish fry.

He used Auntie Doris Beer Batter Recipe.

Reinhold Hoge

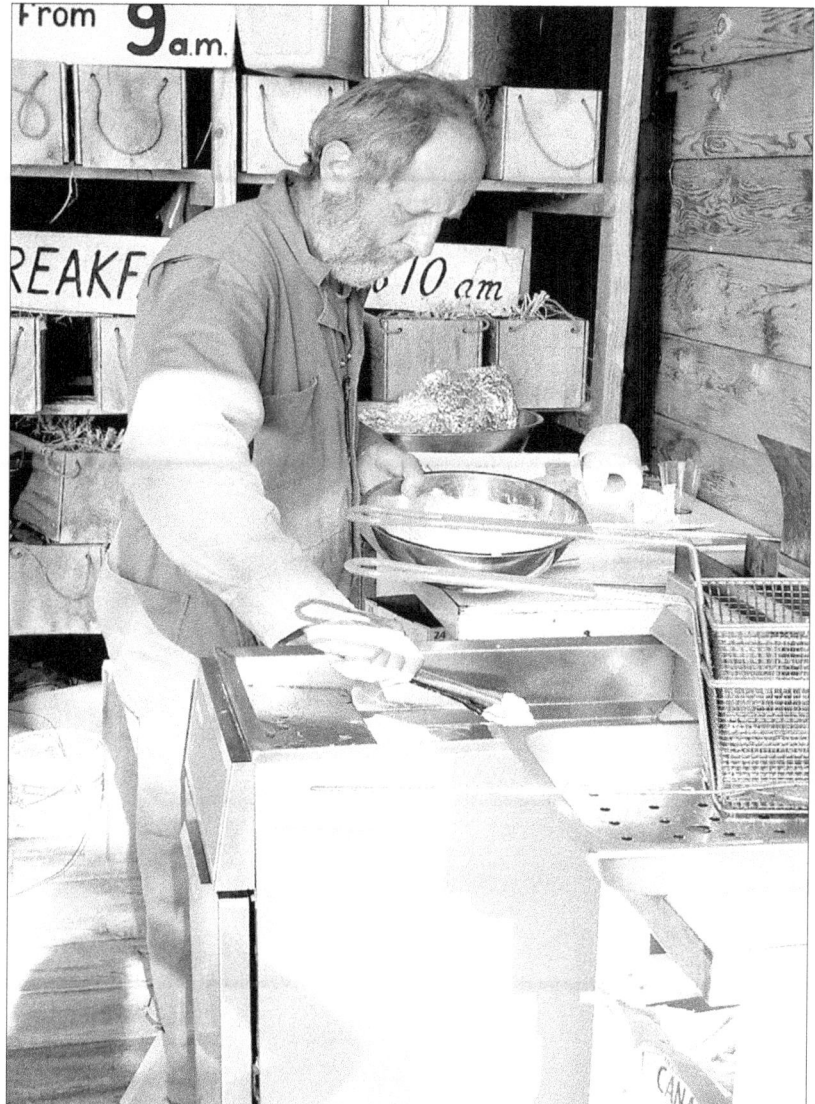

Fish Fry at Reinhold's

53

The Salmon, the Dog & the Cougar

A True Story

It ended with a salmon barbecue, months after the event.

It began with the salmon carried into the house by two triumphant fishermen, male and female. The third member of the procession was Fritzchen, a wire haired dachshund. His squeal alerted the woman near the door. "It's the cougar!" she called out to the family and friend sitting at the dining room table. The owner and friend rushed to the door. The door was slammed. They were both in the house still: the dog's snout was in the cougar's mouth.

The owner yelled, "Let go of my dog!" and kicked the cougar. The cougar complied. But she was trapped! She frantically leapt around the kitchen and living room. Dishes and decorations crashed as she jumped from window to window. The woman worried about the work and cost of broken windows; her mother worried about the mess and looked for a broom to direct the animal back to the door. Her father, a former hunter, tried to whack the frantic animal with his cane as she rushed past where he was seated in front of the fireplace.

The emaciated cougar was dazed after hitting 4 windows. She sat down in front of the old hunter, her head lolling from side to side. The owner got out his rifle. Someone else found the bullets. It was over in little less time than this recounting of the event.

No windows were broken. The terror of the local pussycats was dead.

Fritzchen recovered. The resident pussycat returned 3 weeks later to her again safe house. And, the salmon, cooked to this recipe, was delicious.

(It was much bigger, of course.)

Frieda Home

Barbecued Salmon

2 to 3 pound (1 to 1.5 kg) **salmon fillet**

5 large **garlic** cloves, chopped fine

3 tbsp. (45 ml) fine-chopped **parsley**

3 marinated **sun-dried tomatoes**, chopped fine

1 tsp (5 ml) **salt**

1/4 cup (50 ml) **olive oil**

Combine garlic, parsley, tomatoes, salt and olive oil in jar. Let stand overnight in refrigerator.

Place salmon, skin side down, on large piece of greased foil. Place over low heat on gas barbecue. (I and others don't use foil but others found the fish easier to handle on foil.) Close the top of the barbecue and cook for 10 minutes.

With very sharp knife, cut two lengthwise slits in fillet, dividing the surface of the fish in thirds. Cut to the skin but not through it.

Spread garlic mixture over fillet and into slits. Close top and raise temperature to medium. Cook for an additional 15 minutes or until done.

Makes six to nine servings.

Frieda Home

Frieda Home & Norman Hope

Courtesy of F. Home

Grilled Salmon Burgers

Fresh wild salmon filet cubed (500 grams)

    1/4 cup fresh **coriander**
    1/4 cup minced **red onion**
    2 tbsp grated fresh **ginger root**
    2 tsp **soya sauce**
    4 fresh **Kaiser buns**

Combine all the ingredients above except the buns.

Stir until you have a coarse mixture. Form into four large patties. Shortly before cooking preheat barbeque. Sear patties on grill about four minutes a side turning once until cooked through.

Warm or toast buns, butter and top them off with fresh tomatoes, lettuce and grilled onion slices.

Cathy Campbell

Seed Crust for Fish

    2 tbsp **pumpkin**
    1 tsp **cumin seed**
    1 tsp **coriander seed**
    1 tsp **salt**
    2 tbsp **yoghurt**
    2 tsp **coconut oil**

Toast pumpkin seeds and cumin seeds. Let cool. Coarsely chop then add rest of mixture.

Coat fish with yoghurt then dip fish in crust mixture.

Fry in hot pan with coconut oil for 1 minute on each side.

Bake in a preheated oven 425°F for 5 minutes.

Serve with lemon wedges.

Matt Dixon with salmon.

Louisiana Salmon Fry

Fillet the fish removing skin also. Cut fish up into 2x2 inch cubes. In a bowl, marinade salmon cubes in Louisiana hot sauce. This process firms up the fish.

Coat it in flour by pouring flour in a bag and shaking salmon cubes in the bag next, coating them with flour. Use a cast iron frying pan (which holds the heat). Get it hot with 1/4 inch of oil in it. You have to stand over the pan to over see it.

Fire the salmon pieces in, browning each side by flipping them with a fork.If oil in frying pan isn't hot enough, it will penetrate into the salmon. The last thing you want to do is have the oil soak in the salmon.

When the salmon hits the hot oil, it seals the coating. Keep it rolling and don't overdo cooking. Don't crowd the fish in the frying pan. Place on newspaper to soak up excess oil.

Don Wicks

"The kitchen is a cozy place for living,
visiting & feasting.
A place where ideas are created."

Corrine Corry

Wickaninish Cold Smoked Salmon

The Fish: fillet one medium Chinook salmon (15 to 25 pounds...larger is OK, but smaller fish do not have the requisite fat, and also "cook off" too fast to achieve the desired result) Arrange the fillets on a large platter or cedar plank and sprinkle them with pickling salt, the amount of which to be governed by taste and common sense. The salt will "draw out" water from the fillets, and firm up the flesh. The resultant shrinkage provides an indice of the desired effect. Set the fillets aside for three to five hours in a shady spot, protected from insects, dogs, river otters, crows, etc.

The Smoking Fire: find an old-fashioned Hibachi – the kind with the cast iron grills that can be supported above the briquettes. Light 3 or 4 briquettes in each half of the Hibachi, and when they are reliably aglow, place alder kindling on them. The best – perhaps the only – wood for the desired result is DRY alder, stripped of any bark. Green alder or alder bark lends an undesirable "resinous" taste to the fish. Obviously, there is a tendency for the dry alder kindling to burst into flames, instantly spoiling the desired smoking effect, which brings us to......

The Box: This explains the role of the sheet metal that the Nootka used to closely surround their fire of damp driftwood. It is vital, as soon as the alder is placed on the briquettes, to control the availability of air/oxygen so as to keep it in a smouldering state. Don and I had some chain sawed cedar planks, and Don (he is the artisan of the two of us) built a sturdy box without a "bottom", and supplied with a close-fitting "lid" on top. The height of the box should be at least 5 to 6 inches above the level of the cast iron grills upon which the fillets are placed to "capture" and concentrate the alder smoke, which brings us to........

Place The Fillet(s) On The Grill: And, of course, immediately place the lid on the box, preventing the ignition of the dry alder. What is wanted now are wisps of smoke seeping out from under the lid, which provide visual confirmation that all is well. Small shims may be used to lift the bottom of the box to admit a tiny bit more air if the smoke is dying off. Carefully....oh so carefully. We do not speak of "cooking" time, because the lox quality that is at the core of the Wickaninnish effect is ruined by too much heat or too much time or too little smoke. So the determination of the serving time of the fillets depends mainly upon the delightful phenomenon of semi-viscous white fat of the fillets oozing onto their surface. When that stage frankly announces itself, the fillets are ready to serve. The box is then carefully lifted off the apparatus without disturbing the grills. The fillets can then be shifted from the grill to a platter. This is best carefully done with at least two spatulas, with the aim being to bring the dish to table in one piece. In the case of a large Chinook, two cooks with four spatulas is advised.

Into a run of really BIG Chinooks? One of the beauties of the Wickaninnish approach is that once the central concept is grasped, everything is scalable. Good luck and bon appetit!

John Dixon, Refuge Cove, 2017

Doris' Beer Batter

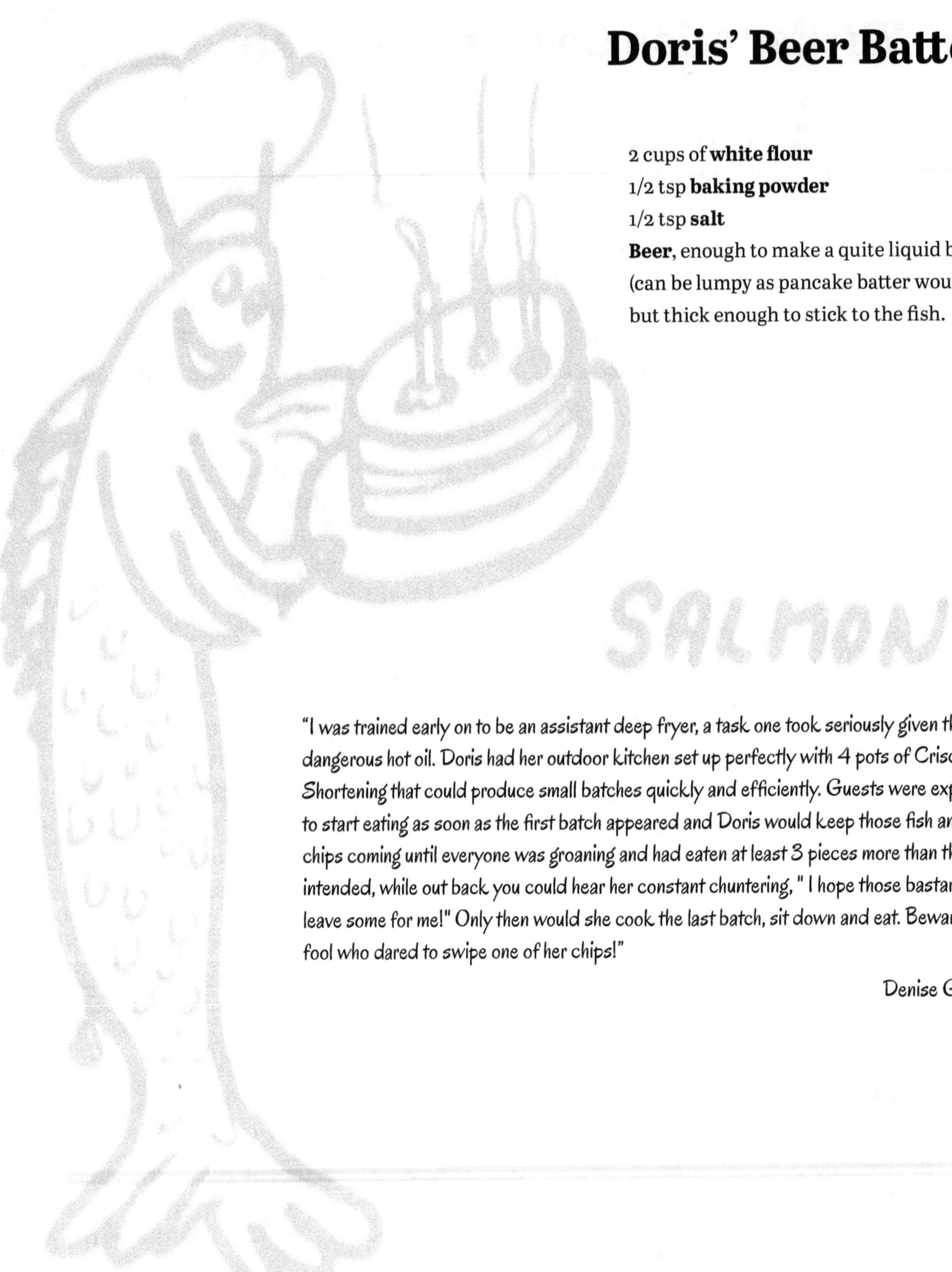

2 cups of **white flour**
1/2 tsp **baking powder**
1/2 tsp **salt**
Beer, enough to make a quite liquid batter
(can be lumpy as pancake batter would be)
but thick enough to stick to the fish.

SALMON

"I was trained early on to be an assistant deep fryer, a task one took seriously given the dangerous hot oil. Doris had her outdoor kitchen set up perfectly with 4 pots of Crisco Shortening that could produce small batches quickly and efficiently. Guests were expected to start eating as soon as the first batch appeared and Doris would keep those fish and chips coming until everyone was groaning and had eaten at least 3 pieces more than they intended, while out back you could hear her constant chuntering, " I hope those bastards leave some for me!" Only then would she cook the last batch, sit down and eat. Beware the fool who dared to swipe one of her chips!"

Denise Gibbons

Doris Hope & Mark Jarvis with a snapper.

Photo courtesy of Judith Williams

Auntie Doris taught anyone who was interested, how to fillet a salmon.

Everyone fished in Desolation Sound as the catch was challenging and plentiful. Famous for her Cod fry, Doris would cook up a feast in the deep fryer set up on the back porch off the kitchen.

Judy and Liz out fishing for ling cod for Auntie Doris' fish fry.

Photo by Judith Williams

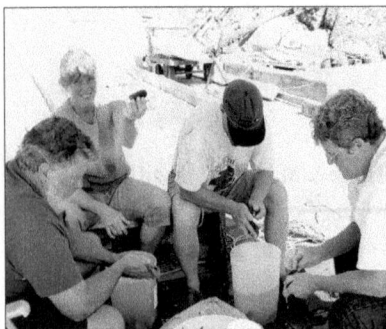
Scrubbing & cleaning
the mussels.

Mussels
A La Meme

Gather mussels (10-20 per person depending on appetites) from a clean water bay away from moorages and docks. Mussels about an inch and a half to 2 inches long are ideal in size to provide a good sized morsel. If mussels are all similar in size the cooking time will be most easily calculated.

Scrub the shells of the mussels with a small brush or a clean plastic scouring pad. Place clean mussels in a mesh bag and hang in clean sea water or place them in a clean bucket of seawater in shade for a few hours to cleanse themselves. Rinse and pull out byssi (the tuft of soft silky filaments that protrude from between the shells) and rinse again. In a deep lidded pot heat 3 tbsp butter and add a few cloves chopped garlic, small bunch of chopped chives or small sweet onion and sauté for a minute to soften.

Add: 2 small leeks or green onions, 1 bay leaf and/or 1 tsp dry herbes de provence or combined available fresh herbs sauté for two more minutes. Add: the mussels sprinkle with salt and pepper. Pour in 1 cup dry white wine cover and simmer gently until the shells open, about 10 minutes.

Remove the mussels into a large serving dish or arrange in individual soup dishes.

The liquid can be reduced and strained directly over the mussels or can be thickened with 3 tbsp butter creamed with 4 tbsp flour sautéed to golden brown, removed from heat with ½ cup of cream whisked in.

Add back into liquid and pour over mussels sprinkled with chopped herbs.

Sandie Ross

Checking for Red Tide TIPS

If the oyster or shellfish has any pink or red do not eat it. You can check for PSP or ASP by rubbing the meat on your lips.
If you get a tingling sensation do not eat them.

You can also feed it to your cat. Check to see if the paws are down its okay.

If they are up forget it. Saltwater parasites die once you react to them but fresh water parasites stay in your system.

Freezing raw seafood kills the parasites.

Tips from a fisherman.

Dinner party in
Sandie`s kitchen.
2003

Oysters for Guests who "Never Touch 'em"

When neither the 'nite bite' nor the dawn beating of the waters produces the trophy salmon for dinner, send your guests to the beach to collect a bucket of oysters.

The main idea behind this recipe is to make palatable to the hesitant guest, fare that is always available ... red tide excepted. And fun can be had if you are game to dive to retrieve them at high tide... especially when the waters have warmed over hot rocks in the afternoon sun.

Large specimens take much less work to produce the necessary poundage to feed a table of holiday makers, but the larger the oyster, the more likely the negative blanching of suntanned faces at the prospect of the texture and the floaty bits.

Shucking oysters is considered to be 'de rigour' on the west coast, but the shells are razor sharp, require a tough glove on the left hand and a sharp oyster knife in your right And tenacity and time.

At the end of a hot afternoon we prefer dumping the whole oysters into a large pasta pot full of boiling water and returning the water to the boil just until the oysters open. Slide a sharp knife along the inside of the shell to sever the two attaching muscles and slide the oyster onto a plate.

The oysters will not be cooked but will have plumped to a firm form that is easily divisible length-wise with a sharp knife.

In a large skillet fry a few slices of bacon for drippings to sauté halved garlic cloves to a golden brown. Remove garlic and set aside with the bacon.

Place enough oysters, cut side down, to fill the bottom of the pan and sauté their bottoms to a crisp brown before turning them to brown the tops. Remove the pan from the heat.

Return crumbled bacon and garlic to the pan to warm with freshly chopped green herbs such as chives, oregano and thyme. Butter may be added and/or olive oil, salt and ground pepper to taste. Lemon wedges for that spritz of citrus.

Serve over pasta, rice or with pan-fried potatoes, a salad on the side. Fresh bread.

Oyster shells can be used to line the paths back to your guests sleeping quarters, to guide them though the dark like small moons gathering the light.

Sandie Ross

TIP FOR OYSTERS:
Freeze for ½ an hour to take the fight out of them before shucking them.

Bouillabaisse

1 day-old French **baguette**, sliced 1 inch thick

2 tbsp **olive oil**

2 cloves **garlic**, peeled and crushed

1 large **onion**, chopped 1 small fennel bulb, thinly sliced

½ cup **fennel** fronds, chopped

1 large pinch **saffron**

1 **bay leaf** ½-inch by 2-inch strip of **orange peel**, orange layer only, white layer scraped away

8-10 very ripe roma **tomatoes** or 14-ounce can whole peeled tomatoes, in juice, chopped 5 cups seafood stock (or 5 teaspoons seafood bouillon with 5 cups water)

1 cup **white wine**

1 tsp **salt**

Some or all of the following seafood, enough to serve 4 to 6 people: mild **white fish** such as halibut, cod, tilapia, or snapper (cut into 1-inch chunks); large **shrimp, lobster** tail chunks, large **crab** legs cut into 1-2 inch lengths, **calamari, clams,** or **mussels**

A large clove of garlic, cut in half crosswise, 1 bunch Italian parsley, chopped.

1. Heat the olive oil in a large, heavy pot over medium heat. Add the crushed garlic, onion, and fennel bulb and sauté until soft but not brown, 5 to 10 minutes.

2. Add the fennel fronds, orange zest, bay leaf, tomatoes, stock or clam juice, wine, and salt. Crumble the saffron threads into the mixture.

3. Bring to a boil over medium-high heat and cook until the vegetables are tender and the liquid is reduced by half, about 20 minutes. Make sure the tomatoes have begun to disintegrate into the broth. Remove the orange peel and the bay leaf.

4. Reduce heat to medium and add the fish (but not shellfish). Cook for about minutes.

5. Add any clams, mussels, lobster, crab, calamari, and shrimp.

6. Cook just until all shells have opened, the shrimp is pink and curled, and the fish flakes easily, about 4 to 6 minutes.

7. Toast the baguette slices. Rub each toasted slice with the cut clove of garlic.

8. Arrange the seafood on the toast slices in soup bowls, and ladle the broth over. Sprinkle with the parsley.

Catherine Gauthier

Shiners are one of the few fish that give birth to their young live.

Photos and recipe from Bill, Diana & Jessi Shillito

FRIED SHINERS
- FISH FOR SHINERS UNDER THE REFUGE COVE DOCK RAMP USING A HERRING JIG
- BAIT HOOKS WITH SMALL PIECES OF WIENER FROM THE REFUGE COVE STORE.
- PUT THE SHINERS IN A BUCKET OF SEA WATER WHILE FISHING.
- KEEP THE BIGGEST AND THROW THE REST BACK, FOR FUTURE FISHING DAYS.
- REMOVE HEADS AND ENTRAILS.
- IN A PLASTIC BAG, MIX FLOUR, PEPPER, SPIKE AND GARLIC POWDER.
- PUT MOIST FISH IN BAG AND SHAKE WELL.
- FRY TILL GOLDEN BROWN IN HOT BUTTER.
  - ENJOY.

Prawns (Bugs) Lime Coconut

1 can **coconut milk**

1 tbsp of **chili** paste (Sambal)

Prawns freshly caught

Handful of **cilantro**

Fresh **lime juice**

Behead and skin prawns. Set aside head and skins for prawn stock. Sauté prawns for 30 seconds in olive oil.

Fold in coconut milk and chili paste. Add freshly squeezed lime juice.

Add finely chopped basil.

Cathy JC

In the summer the lowest tides are in the daytime.
In winter the lowest tides are at night when one can pick sack fulls of clams.
There are many long clam beaches along the coast but most of them were all dug up by 1935.

If you hang them between the float logs they will be good to eat for two weeks.
It also helps to get rid of the sand.

You can hang mussels, oysters & prawns off the dock for a few days to keep them fresh.

Hand painted fabric art of Sharon with prawns by Mary Ruzich.

Tim at Oyster Lease, Center Island.

Oysters with Linguine

2 cups heavy **cream**

a dozen **oysters**, shucked

1 tbsp **garlic** (minced)

3 tbsp **Creole seasoning**

½ tsp **salt**

2 tbsp ground **pepper**

½ lb **linguini**

1 oz **caviar**

2 green **onions**

Heat the cream, garlic, salt, Creole seasoning, pepper and oysters until the seafood is done.

Keep the heat low.

Cook the linguini the usual way drain the water, and top with cream sauce, more pepper, caviar & green onions.

Creole Seasoning

Stir together

2 ½ tbsp **paprika**

2 tbsp **salt**

2 tbsp **garlic** powder

1 tbsp **onion** powder

1 tbsp **cayenne** pepper

1 tbsp dried **oregano**

1 tbsp **thyme**

Frances Hill

(Gordie Sheridan's recipe)

67

Baked Salmon

one whole **salmon** clean and slit open

¾ cup melted **butter**

2 tbsp **liquid soy seasoning** or **Japanese soy**

1 tbsp each of herbs fresh or dried **tarragon, basil, rosemary**

2 cloves of chopped **garlic**

1 tbsp salted **lemon juice** and 2 tbsp chopped up **lemon rind**

2 tbsp of **maple syrup** drizzled on top

Mix this filling together and spread on both sides inside of salmon. Close up.

Wrap in foil and bake at 350 on grill or in oven for 45 minutes. Cool for 15 minutes.

Salted Lemon

Quarter lemons and squish down with a wooden spoon into a small canning jar with coarse salt on the bottom. Sprinkle judiciously with kosher salt on top. Shake it up every now and then to keep the juices distributed evenly. Let sit on counter for 3 days then refrigerate.

This is a delicious condiment to add to salad dressings, yoghurt dips, and marinated cheese, baking chicken and seafoods.

Happy Hour Chiang Mai Clams

*C*heck for shellfish closures.

Take a friend, go to your favourite clam beach and dig up about 150 small to medium clams.

Rinse the clams and hang them in the water for a couple of days to let them flush.

Steam them open, saving the liquid for chowder. Take them out of the shells.

Let them cool in a bowl while you have your pre-Happy Hour nap.

Heat oil to a hot temperature in a large frying pan.

Throw in one clam. If it gives a good loud sizzle the oil's hot enough.

Throw in the rest of the clams.

Shake the pan frequently. When it looks like some of the clams are turning brown, pour in some well-shaken Chiang Mai sauce. Our favourite brand is, *As You Like It*.

Stir the hot clams with the Chiang Mai sauce for a minute or two.

Issue toothpicks to everyone and serve in the pan. Our friends will consume 20 to 25 clams each.

These will go well with your libation of choice.

Submitted by Bill Lea aboard *Ruxton Point*

SOUPS
&
CHOWDERS

Sandie and Alister crossing Lewis Channel to Refuge Cove with MV *Seapod* loaded full with provisions. 1998

Judy's Butter Clam Chowder

Amelia's Cat House Clams

Split butter clamshells and bodies with a knife, drain raw, and dip the open side into butter.

Fry half a clam batter side down, on a griddle.

Procure clams by digging, Open live clams raw, save nectar and remove siphons.

Sauté three slices of chopped gammon bacon and drain. Add one cup of chopped onion, three or four cubed carrots, and two cubed large potatoes and turn in gammon fat. Pour in to pot, two cups of clam nectar and a cup of water. Add one cup chopped celery halfway through. Cook until vegetables soften.

Lightly mash a third of the vegetables leaving lots of lumps. Potato starch will thicken the chowder.

Add chunked clam bodies to pot. Bring gently to a boil, turn down heat and add one cup of milk. Heat but do not boil.

Ladle into bowls. Slide one tbsp. of cream over top and sprinkle with finely chopped fresh parsley. Pepper to taste.

Do not on any account add salt.

You may add 1/2 pound snapper chunks during the last heating. To use horse clams, blanch the neck, remove the black covering and chop finely.

This recipe was bases on Norm Hope's Clam Chowder.

From Judith Williams' book "Clam Gardens"

Oyster Bisque

16 **oysters**, shucked

1 cup **clam juice**

1 tbsp hot **water**

1/4 tsp **saffron** threads, crushed

1 tsp **butter**

1 cup chopped **red onion**

1/8 tsp **cayenne**

1 cup chopped **celery**

1/4 cup **flour**

1/4 tsp ground **coriander**

3 cups **milk**

1/4 chopped **parsley**

1/4 tsp **salt**

Coarsely chop oysters. Combine water and saffron in a small bowl and set aside. Melt the butter in a large saucepan over medium heat. Add the onion & celery Cook for 5 minutes, stirring frequently.

Stir in flour and coriander; cook for 1 minute. Add the clam juice, saffron water and milk, stirring with whisk. Cook until thick (about 12 minutes), stirring frequently. Add the oysters, parsley, salt and cayenne. Cook for 3 minutes until edges of oysters curl. Yield: 6 one-cup servings.

Jackie Frioud

Jackie Frioud makes salt-glazed, functional pottery. Thrown on the wheel and salt-fired in a gas kiln, Jackie aims for a sturdy elegance in her ceramics that combines beauty and mindfulness with sensible, everyday function.

"We often had community dinners and I particularly remember the clam chowder that Don, a younger single fellow, I think, made. As we don't eat clams, he was kind enough to set aside some chowder before he put the clams in at the end. It was a wonderful soup."

Anne Melul

Sophie Jarvis at the store.

Pacific Oyster Stew

"I've had quite a history with oysters. In the 1940's I hated them, mostly because my parents served the smoked oysters as hors d'oeuvres and they grossed me out.

Then in the 1950's my family would come up to Desolation Sound in the summer and mom started frying them with crumbs and butter. Those were pretty good.

Then I had quite an absence from oysters until the 1970's when my boss in Terrace had a friend bring fresh oysters up by plane when he came up on business. They were very pricey but good.

Then we moved to Refuge and I thought I was in heaven. All the oysters I could eat on the beach in front of the house. With the advent of the trend toward healthy eating,. We still indulge in fried oysters off and on but find this recipe is a delicious alternative"

Julia

Ingredients: Note the saffron isn't cheap but it really makes a difference. I left it out once and realized it's pungent flavor was key to the recipe. I powdered it with a mortar and pestle.

- 4 slices **bacon** chopped into ½" pieces
- 1 medium **onion** or **leek** chopped
- 2 garlic cloves minced
- ½ tsp grated fresh **ginger**
- 2 **celery** stalks including tops sliced
- 4 medium **carrots** cut into ½" slices
- 3 cups of **water**
- 1 cube **vegetable bouillon**
- 1 tsp **Worcestershire sauce**
- ½ tsp **saffron**, ground
- 1 medium red Pontiac **potato** cubed
- 2 cups **oysters** including liquor (the recipe was using small oysters – if mine were large I cut them into bite size pieces)
- 6 oz. 2% evaporated **milk**
- 1 tbsp. **cornstarch**

Method: In a large pot, fry bacon on medium heat until golden brown Sauté the onion, garlic, and grated ginger with the bacon for a further 2 minutes

Add celery for one minute, then carrots and cook for a further two minutes

Add water, bouillon, Worcestershire sauce, saffron & potato and simmer until potato is almost cooked

Add the oysters, bring to a boil and simmer for 5 minutes

Stir the cornstarch into the evaporated milk and slowly pour this into the oyster mixture while continuously stirring Bring this just to the boil, remove from the heat and serve with fresh hot cornbread.

Julia & Doug Allen

Autumn Pumpkin Squash Soup

Make 10 cups stock from a Halloween pumpkin or garden squash by cutting up and roasting in oven for 45 minutes.

Cool carve out flesh and discard skin.

Throw flesh in a big pot.

Sauté a leek, garlic cloves & green pepper in a little butter then add to pot.

Blend in grated fresh ginger root, cilantro, sage and grated orange zest. (to taste)the last few minutes of cooking.

Add ½ tsp chipotle sauce for spice.

Add a cup of coconut milk

Top with chopped mint or toasted pumpkin seeds.

Add fresh shredded spinach, carrots, barley, lime pickle to soup layers to vary the flavour.

Cathy Campbell

To make an easy job of roasting squash, pumpkin, cut in half lengthwise, scrape out the seeds and place cut side down on an oiled baking tray.

Bake in a 375° oven until the fork pierces easily through the flesh. Cool and scoop out the soft flesh.

Surprise baby shower gathering for Sarah and Marina May. May 2011

John & Janet Ellis on the "Hemie"
so named because it was built
out of hemlock.

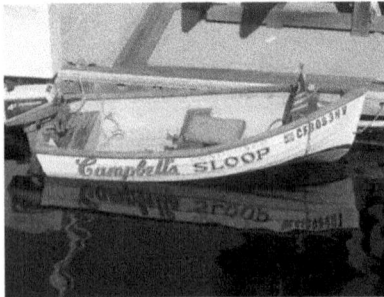

Seafood Chowder

To 1½ c boiling water add:

1 c chopped celery
1 c chopped onion
1½ c cubed potatoes

When tender, add one chowder pack
except lobster. Cook slowly 10-15 min
chop scallops & shrimp before adding

Add:
1½ c milk   Pepper
1 tsp Margarine   Seafood seasoning
Salt

Stir in:
1 can mushrooms drained
1 can cream of celery soup
1 can cream of mushroom soup
add lobster meat chopped fine.
Stir. Let sit in cool place 2-4 hours

You can use lobster or crab flavoured
crack.

J Ellis

SALAD &
VEGETABLE
DISHES

Refuge Cove group picture in front of the school house. 1976

Photo by Denise Gibbons

Blueberry Sauce

Great with Salmon

1 cup **blueberries**
¾ cups **shallots**
Garlic clove thinly sliced
¼ tsp coarse **salt**
1/8 tsp allspice
¼ cup water
1 tbsp **balsamic vinegar**

Sauté shallots, garlic, spices then add water, blueberries and balsamic vinegar.

Mash and thicken.

Serve warm with fresh black pepper.

RICE CASS.   ANNE M.

2 large onions, chopped
½ c. salad oil
2 fresh tomatoes, peeled + chopped
4 c. water
2 tsp salt
¼ tsp. pepper
2 c rice
1 can garbanzo beans.

Saute onion in oil until golden brown. Add tomatoes, water, salt and pepper and bring to a boil. Add rice and garbanzos. Cover and simmer approx. 20 min. Serves 6-8

Anne and Albert Mulel and son Mark lived on Corrine's site in the early days of the co-op. She taught the kids for two years.

Recipe written by Anne Melul.

Photo courtesy of Denise Gibbons

Fast and Furious Vegetable Recipe

It just takes a few minutes to prepare. I don't do meat anymore but when I used to do I would cook it in an enamel cast iron roaster.

No spices, no junk.

Roast in the propane oven at 350 °F for one hour

Add 1 cup water in the bottom

Put the dry stuff in bottom of pot – Chickpeas

In steamer put vegetables

Cabbage segmented cut out root carrots, winter potatoes with skin left on

Cut up Bok Choy, cut up roots, chard greens, beet tops and layer greens on top of heavier vegetables

Slice up everything in your hand as it saves cleaning the cutting board.

Just don't put my name on it 'cause I don't want a path bitten to my door.

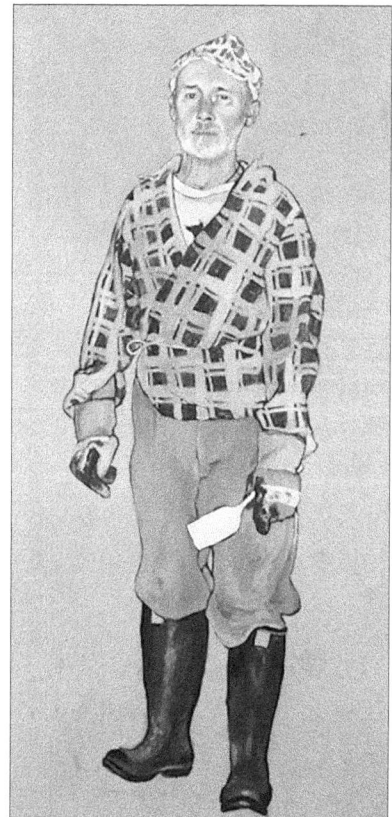

Sauce for Vegetables

   1/2 cup **orange** juice
   1/4 cup **soy sauce**
   2–3 **cloves** minced garlic
   1 tbsp grated fresh **ginger**
   1-2 tbsp **honey**
   2 tsp **sesame oil**
   2 tbsp **cornstarch**

Mix first 6 ingredients. Place cornstarch in a bowl whisk the liquid mixture into it.

Set aside and whisk again before adding to sautéed vegetables.

Nettles

Harvest tender nettles in the early spring as the plants emerge in mineral rich areas in old growth forest floors.

Collect with plastic bags or heavy duty berry picking gloves on otherwise you will get strung.

Cut in the spring when tender.

Steam them

Add butter, salt & pepper to taste.

The best antidote for stings is to soak in nettle tea.

Nettle tea is packed full of minerals and iron.

Dried and crushed they can be added to fresh pasta, soups, breads and tea.

Nettles are a delicious addition to lasagne.

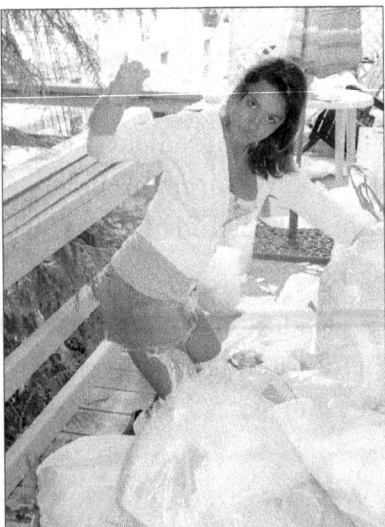

Found this recipe for Caesar Salad Dressing in Doris Hope's cabin.

Ariel hard at work recycling.

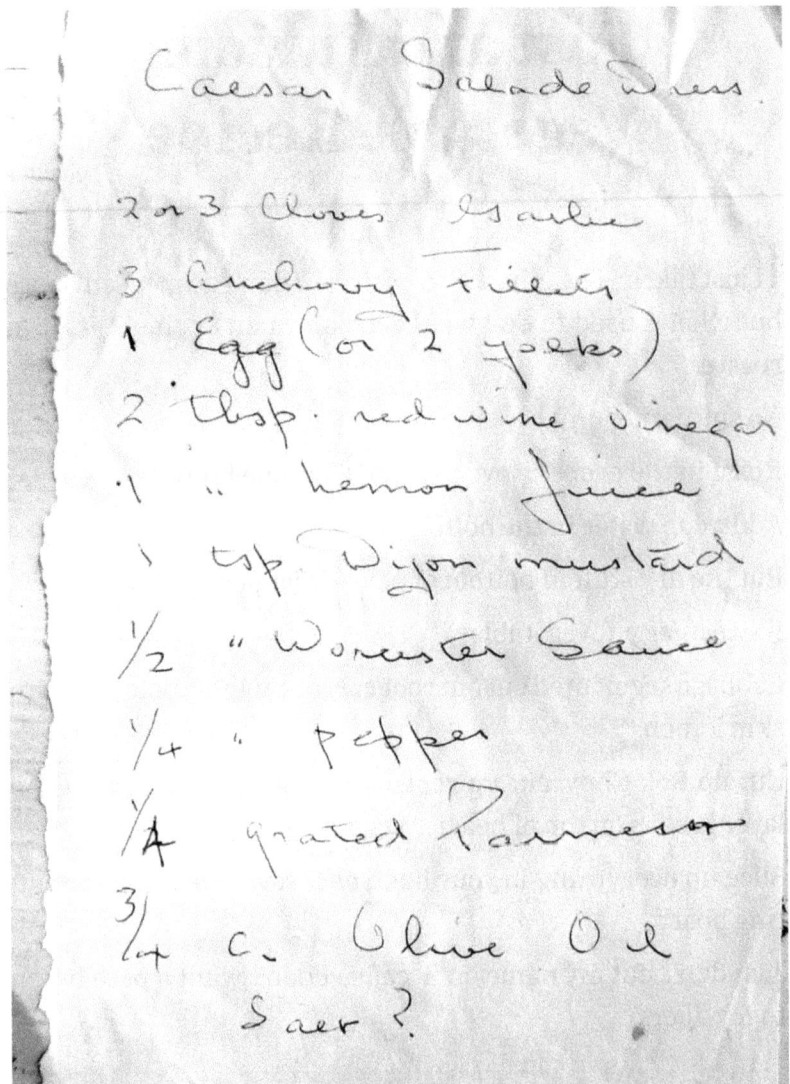

Russian Vegetarian Pie

4 **eggs**

1 1/4 cups all-purpose **flour**

1 teaspoon **white sugar**

1 teaspoon **salt**

3 tablespoons **butter**

4 ounces **cream cheese**, softened

2 tablespoons **butter**

1 **onion**, chopped

1 small head **cabbage**, shredded

1/8 teaspoon dried **marjoram**

1/8 teaspoon dried **tarragon**

1/4 teaspoon dried **basil** leaves

salt and **pepper** to taste

1 tablespoon **butter**

8 ounces fresh **mushrooms**, sliced

4 ounces **cream cheese**, softened

1/2 teaspoon dried **dill** weed

Preheat oven to 400 degrees F (200 degrees C.) Place eggs in a saucepan and cover with cold water. Bring water to a boil and immediately remove from heat. Cover and let eggs stand in hot water for 10 to 12 minutes. Remove from hot water, cool, peel and slice.

In a large bowl, combine flour, sugar and salt. Cut in butter until mixture resembles coarse crumbs. Stir in cream cheese until mixture forms a ball. Roll out 2/3 of the pastry and line a 9 inch pie dish. Roll out the remaining pastry and make a circle large enough to cover the dish. Put it away to chill.

In a large skillet, melt about 2 tablespoons butter. Add the onion and cabbage and sauté for several minutes, stirring constantly. Season to taste with marjoram, tarragon, and basil, salt and pepper. Cook, stirring occasionally, until the cabbage is wilted and the onions are soft. Remove from the pan and set aside. Add a couple tablespoons of butter to the pan and sauté the mushrooms lightly for about 5 to 6 minutes, stirring constantly.

Spread the softened cream cheese in the bottom of the pie shell. Arrange the egg slices in a layer over the cheese. Sprinkle them with chopped dill, and then cover them with the cabbage. Make a final layer of the sautéed mushrooms and cover with the circle of pastry. Seal and flute the edges of the crust. With a sharp knife, cut a few short slashes through the top crust.

Bake in the preheated oven for 15 minutes. Reduce temperature to 350 degrees F (175 degrees C) and bake for 20 to 25 minutes, or until golden brown.

Dave Cartwright with his cat L'il Bit.

"After a long winter of eating root vegetables a body craves anything green. Greens from the garden, bush and sea, stinging nettles, goose grass, glasswort snipped rinsed and boiled is a welcome addition on the plate. I collect all summer long. Dorothy Thomas used to collect also.

I collect Ulva seaweed and sea lettuce in abundance in my kayak, hang it out to dry on a line in the sun then roast it in the oven or toast it in a cast iron pan briefly to completely dry it out. Cool . Store in a dry glass jar in a dark place."

Cathy Campbell

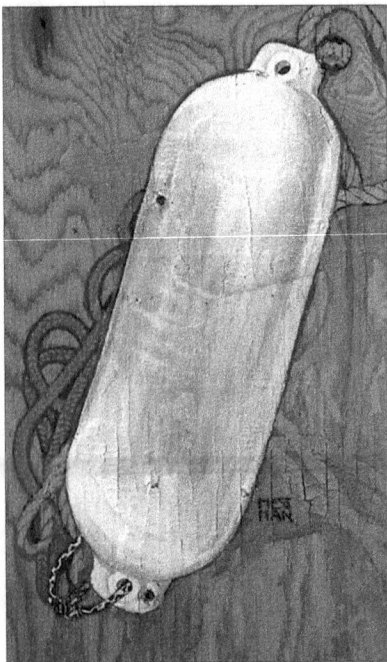

Sea Asparagus Salad

Also known as Chicken claws, glasswort

Salicornia Pacifica ¾ lb pacific samphire.

2 tbsp chop **olives**

1 hard boiled **egg**

Cherry tomatoes halved

Or sauté in **butter** with grated **carrots** and chopped **mint**

Steam **asparagus** and chill in marinade of

½ cup **olive oil**

5 tbsp **lemon juice**

1 tsp **sugar**

½ tsp **salt**

½ tsp **paprika**

½ tsp **mustard** and a dash of **cayenne**.

Top with wild onions with the pink flowertops sautéed lightly with olive oil .

A great addition is potato a potato salad topped with grated carrots.

Spinach and Avocado Salad

Wash and spin dry spinach leaves. Chop green onion. Toss. Slice up avocado and arrange on top. Top with sunflower, pumpkin and pomegranate seeds.

Dressing

½ tsp orange zest

½ tsp/lime zest

¼ cup orange juice

2 tbsp lime juice

1 tbsp olive oil

¼ tsp chili powder

Salt and pepper to taste

Cathy Campbell

Susan's Sunshine Salad

Carrots
1 **orange**
Raisins
½ **apple** (optional)
Mayonnaise

Peel and grate carrots. Peel orange, separate into wedges and cut into small chunks. Add raisins. Grate and add apple if desired.

Mix in mayonnaise to taste, or eat as is. Top with roasted sesame seeds.

Susan Lea

PESTO with Zesto

You can make pesto with any herb in your garden.

Cilantro, basil, coriander, chives, dill, fennel arugula, pea blossoms and nasturtium Great tasting on top of a pasta, potatoes, quinoa & salads.

Make a pesto paste with garlic scaps, basil, garlic, walnuts or sunflower seeds.

Dressing

½ cup sweet **chilli** sauce
2 tbsp rice wine **vinegar**
1 tbsp grated fresh **ginger**

Citrus fruit helps digest carciferous vegetables like broccoli, spinach, chard and kale.

Cranberry Salsa

3 cups fresh or **frozen cranberrie**s
2/3 cup **dried cranberries**
¼ cup finely chopped **red onion**
Bunch of fresh **cilantro**
1 **orange** or frozen **orange juice**
Maple syrup

Process or chop up very coarsely.

Stir in dried cranberries and chop up into small bits.

Top with chopped cilantro.

You can substitute with any fresh berries.

Add finely chopped crystallized ginger or a pinch of crushed red pepper flakes to the salsa to taste.

Quinoa Salad

1 cup of **quinoa**, rinsed
2 cups of **water** or **stock**
1 medium **red onion**, chopped
3 cloves **garlic**, chopped
1/4 cup chopped fresh **basil** or **cilantro**
1/4 cup chopped fresh **coriander** (cilantro)
1 **red pepper** chopped up
1 can or fresh corn **kernels**
4 tbsp **lime** juice
3 tsp **olive oil**
3 cups shredded romaine **lettuce**
1 **avocado**, cubed lime juice
1 tbsp chopped toasted **pumpkin seeds**
sea salt and **pepper**, to taste
Spices to add ½ tsp of **cumin, paprika** and **turmeric**

Bring water/ stock to a rolling boil then add quinoa. Cover with lid and simmer gently on low heat for about 15 minutes. If you have a rice cooker you can prepare same as rice. Fluff with fork and transfer to a bowl.

Sauté garlic and onions until tender then add corn and red pepper until lightly toasted.

For a nuttier flavour, add quinoa to pan and lightly toast it with the red pepper and corn. Add chopped herbs, 2 tsp lime juice,1 tsp olive oil, salt and pepper.

Toss romaine in a dressing of 2 tbsp lime juice and 2 tbsp olive oil. Season with salt and cracked black pepper.

Serve quinoa on the bed of salad greens.

Add sliced avocado on top.

Sprinkle with chopped toasted pumpkin seeds.

Serve in bowls on side for additional toppings of chopped cilantro and fresh sliced papaya.

Cathy J Campbell

Baked Kale Chips

Pick kale, chard or beet greens

Wash well, then spin or pat dry

Cut out any thick stalks

Place in a plastic bag & toss with 1-2 tbsp. olive oil

Place eaves on cookie sheet spread apart

Sprinkle with salt

Bake in oven 350°F for 30 minutes turning leaves 1/2 way through until they are crisp.

These are a great appetizer for any type of seafood meal.

I also found that they go stale quickly (like if you don't eat them all in one sitting) but can be "refreshed" by putting them back in the oven for 5-10 minutes, or can be frozen wrapped in paper towel.

Top with cashews or engevita yeast flakes.

Mary Ruzich

Sesame Tahini Dressing

½ cup **tahini**
¼ cup **lime** or **lemon** juice
1 tsp Dijon **mustard**
1 clove chopped **garlic**
2 tbsp **tamari** or **soya** sauce
½ tsp **pepper**
½ cup **water**

Salal Berry Dressing

Salal berries mashed up.

Olive oil

Rice wine vinegar, or white wine vinegar

Tossed salad greens, or baby spinach

Add fresh tangerine slices strawberries to salad.

Top with toasted pumpkin seeds.

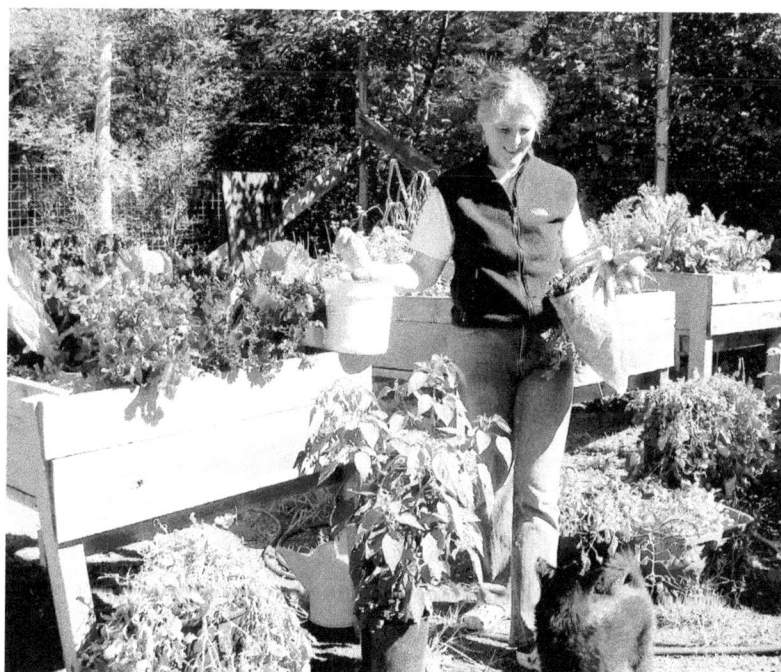

Mary in her abundant vegetable garden.

Corrine & Spencer out for a row.

Ernie & Lena, Norm & Doris enjoying a
meal outside Reinhold's kitchen.
Photo by Frieda Home

Sauerkraut recipe written
by Lena Hoge. 1974

Mushroom Nut Veggie Burgers

One small loaf of cornmeal bread (I have substituted with cooked couscous, tabouli or raw soaked oatmeal) – if I don't have enough cornbread left over.

Add the equivalent of finely chopped up:

½ head of **celery/kale** or **swiss chard**

One cup of **mushrooms** finely chopped

6 green **onions** all finely chopped up

1 clove **garlic** crushed

½ tbsp. **tarragon**, celery seeds

Finally chopped walnuts, almond slivers, sunflower seeds, hemp seeds (whatever nuts you have)

Season with tamari sauce & balsamic (a few sprinkles of each)

Blend together 3 eggs – more if needed to make it sticky

Mix it all together and form your patties.

Cook in coconut oil on high heat, flip over to seal each side. Lower temperature to medium heat and continue heating through until firm.

They freeze very well. Separate with parchment paper for individual servings.

Enjoy!
Cathy Campbell

Jungle phones at Refuge Cove were a handy source of communication. Unfortunately, they stopped working over a decade ago and have been unable to get them going again.

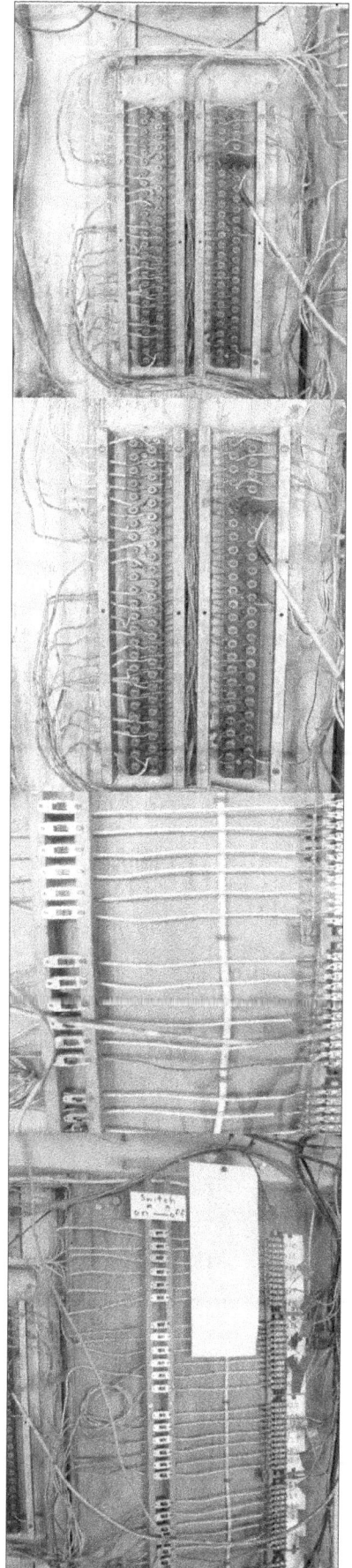

Cookie recipes written by Dorothy Thomas, are from a plastic bag of food related notes and clippings given by her daughter Betty Yexex to Judy when she was clearing out the house in the Hole. They were written in a steno notebook dated 1961 when she was cooking at a Logging camp in Ramsey Arm.

Chocolate Cookies

Cream together
½ cup shortening
½ cup. c.p. brown sugar
¼ cup white sugar

add:
1 Beaten egg
1½ squares chocolate (melted) 3 Tblsp Cocoa
1 tsp Vanilla
Beat thoroly
sift together.
1½ cups flour
½ tsp baking powder
½ tsp salt.

Bake 5 to 6 min 375
for Variety add ½ cup chopped
nuts or m cherries

Desserts

Detail of watercolour painting of Dorothy Thomas. Judith Williams. 1986

Honey Cake

My husband Ken and I first sailed into Refuge Cove in the early 70's in our 28 ft. boat "Happiness Is".

We met Alan and Sylvia Fogg and family about 1975 in Cortez Bay with their boat "Kismet".

We continued to visit the Cove in our 38 ft. boat "Sea Urchin" and also to visit Alan when he was working there.

We often enjoyed Reinhold's burgers and his honey was a welcome ingredient in my cooking. A one pound jar is needed for this delicious cake.

Topping ¾ cup **sugar**

1 cup **oatmeal**

¼ cup flaked **coconut**

½ cup **margarine**

¾ cup **chopped nuts**

¼ cup of **margarine** or **butter**

1 ½ cups **flour**

2 **eggs**

1/3 cup of **honey**

1 ½ teaspoons **salt**

1 cup of boiling **water**

½ tsp **ginger**

3 tsp **baking powder**

¼ tsp **cloves**

1 cup **honey**

1 tsp **cinnamon**

½ tsp **nutmeg**

Method: In roomy bowl, cover margarine with oatmeal and pour over them the cup of boiling water. Let stand for 20 minutes. Add eggs and honey, then stir in dry ingredients. Pour into 8 inch square pan and bake in a 325 °F oven for an hour or until it tests done.

Cream margarine and honey for topping together and mix in nuts and coconut. Broil in oven until melted.

The first time I made this I didn't have an oven. I used an old 5 quart pressure cooker with the gaskets removed. Heated it up on the propane stove and used a 10 inch tube pan for the cake batter. Worked great and the tube became a handle to lift out with.

Pat Kirkham (Championship)

Jim Lusse & Allen Fogg

Two Standard Cakes

The ingredients for these easy and delicious cakes can be found in my pantry.

Poppy seed

1 pkg. **yellow cake mix**

1 pkg. instant **vanilla** pudding

4 **eggs**

3/4 cup **oil**

3/4 cup **dry sherry**

1 tsp grated **nutmeg**

1/4 cup **poppy seeds**

Chocolate Whisky

1 pkg **chocolate cake mix**

1 pkg instant **chocolate pudding**

4 **eggs**

3/4 cup **oil**

1/4 cup cold strong **coffee**

1/2 cup **whiskey**

For each cake, mix all ingredients in a large bowl. Pour into a greased ring mould/ Bundt pan and bake at 350 °F for 30 minutes or until done.

Mary Ruzich

Household Hints

To test oven temperatures without a thermometer sprinkle a tsp of flour on an inverted pie plate or baking tin and place in heated oven.

If flour turns delicate brown in five minutes the temperature is low, 250 to 325 F.

If flour turns golden brown in five minutes the temperature is moderate, 325 to 400 F.

If flour turns deep brown in five minutes the temperature is hot, 400 to 450 F.

Mum's Chocolate Cake

My mother Edna's famous chocolate cake– I made hundreds of times at Refuge! Always a favourite.

> 2 tablespoons of **butter**
> 1 cup white **sugar**
> 1 **egg**
> 1 teaspoon **vanilla**
> 1 cup **flour**
> 1/2 tsp baking **soda**
> 1 tsp **baking powder**
> 1/4 tsp **salt**
> 4 heaping tablespoons Fry's **cocoa**
> 1 scant cup boiling **water** (little less than a cup)

Cream together butter and sugar, then add egg and vanilla.

Sift together flour, soda, baking powder, salt in separate bowl.

Mix cocoa and boiling water, dissolving lumps.

Pour half of dry mixture into butter bowl, beat well. Add half of cocoa liquid, then remaining flour, then liquid.

Beat well till mixed.

Pour into 8 inch greased round or square pan. Bake at 325°F for 30 minutes.

This recipe works well to double or triple size. I usually ice it with a butter icing made with a very strong shot of espresso for the liquid.

Denise Gibbons

"Denise looked through all her cherished recipes for one from Doris Hope. She wrote "Sadly I have nothing from Doris. She never used a recipe except for the Tender flake Pastry which she taught me to use. Every Christmas we'd spend a day making mince tarts– always cutting the mincemeat with applesauce & a few spoonfuls of flour to make it go farther. Almost forgot—we always added a good swig of rum also."

Denise

MOM'S CHOCLATE CAKE
2 tbsp. margarine or butter
1 Cup white sugar
1 tsp. vanilla
1 egg
1 cup flour
1 tsp. baking powder
½ " " soda
½ " salt
4 tbsp. (heaping) Fry's cocoa.
1 scant cup boiling water.

The Plain Cake

Bake in a round 8" x 4" greased and floured pan @ 300°F slowly – for 1 1/2 to 2 hours.

MIX:

2 cups **flour**

1 cup **sugar**

Rub in well 1/2 cup of **butter**

Separately measure 1 cup currants and 1 cup raisins.

At this point 1/4 c chopped mixed peel can be added.

I don't like peel so instead I shake in some dried lemon peel and dried orange peel if I can find it.

Flour this mixture well to keep the fruit mixed throughout the cake.

Stir in this fruit mix to the flour, sugar and butter.

Beat 2 or 3 eggs to the colour of lemon.

To the flour mixture add the eggs, a splash of milk-variable, a good large splash of brandy and 1 teaspoon of baking soda dissolved in a tablespoon of water.

1/4 tsp. salt can be added but I don't.

I also splash in some lemon juice concentrate and about a tablespoon of frozen thawed, if possible orange juice.

I have used scotch instead of brandy now and then but I believe brandy makes a better cake.

Stir well. Add more milk if needed.

The batter should be the consistency of a pancake batter.

If it is too wet just cook it longer.

Test with a straw in the middle for doneness.

It may dome and crack on top.

Anne Ferguson

"Doris was very fond of a family cake that I would make for her. My mother made this cake once a week for 50 years! It is an old North England recipe and the quantities used vary according to their availability."

Anne Ferguson

Helpful Hint

To get a smooth clean cut when slicing a cake, run a large knife blade under very hot water.

Pat dry with a clean cloth and slice.

A gift to Refuge Cove Store from Nancy and Ray Kendal.

BASE

> 2 squares semi-sweet **chocolate**
>
> One half cup unsalted **butter**
>
> 2 tablespoons **sugar**
>
> One quarter teaspoon **vanilla**
>
> 2 cups graham cracker **crumbs**
>
> 1 cup flaked **coconut**
>
> One half cup **walnuts**, finely chopped

FILLING

> One quarter cup unsalted **butter**, softened
>
> 3 tablespoons **milk**
>
> 2 cups powdered **sugar**
>
> 2 tablespoons Bird's Custard Powder OR ½ teaspoon **vanilla** and 2 tablespoons **cornstarch**

GLAZE

> 4 squares semi-sweet **chocolate**
>
> 1 tablespoon unsalted **butter**

Nanaimo Bars

BASE: Melt chocolate and butter together in a double boiler over hot, not boiling water. Add remaining base ingredients and mix thoroughly. Press into the bottom of a 9 x 13 pan and chill until firm.

FILLING: Cream the butter. Add ½ of the powdered sugar and cream until smooth. Add the milk and custard powder (or vanilla and cornstarch) and stir to combine. Add remaining powdered sugar and combine thoroughly until smooth and creamy. Spread evenly over the base layer and chill at least 15 minutes.

GLAZE: Melt the chocolate and butter together in the top of a double boiler over hot, not boiling, water. Spread over the filling layer. Chill. Cut into bars.

Catherine Gauthier

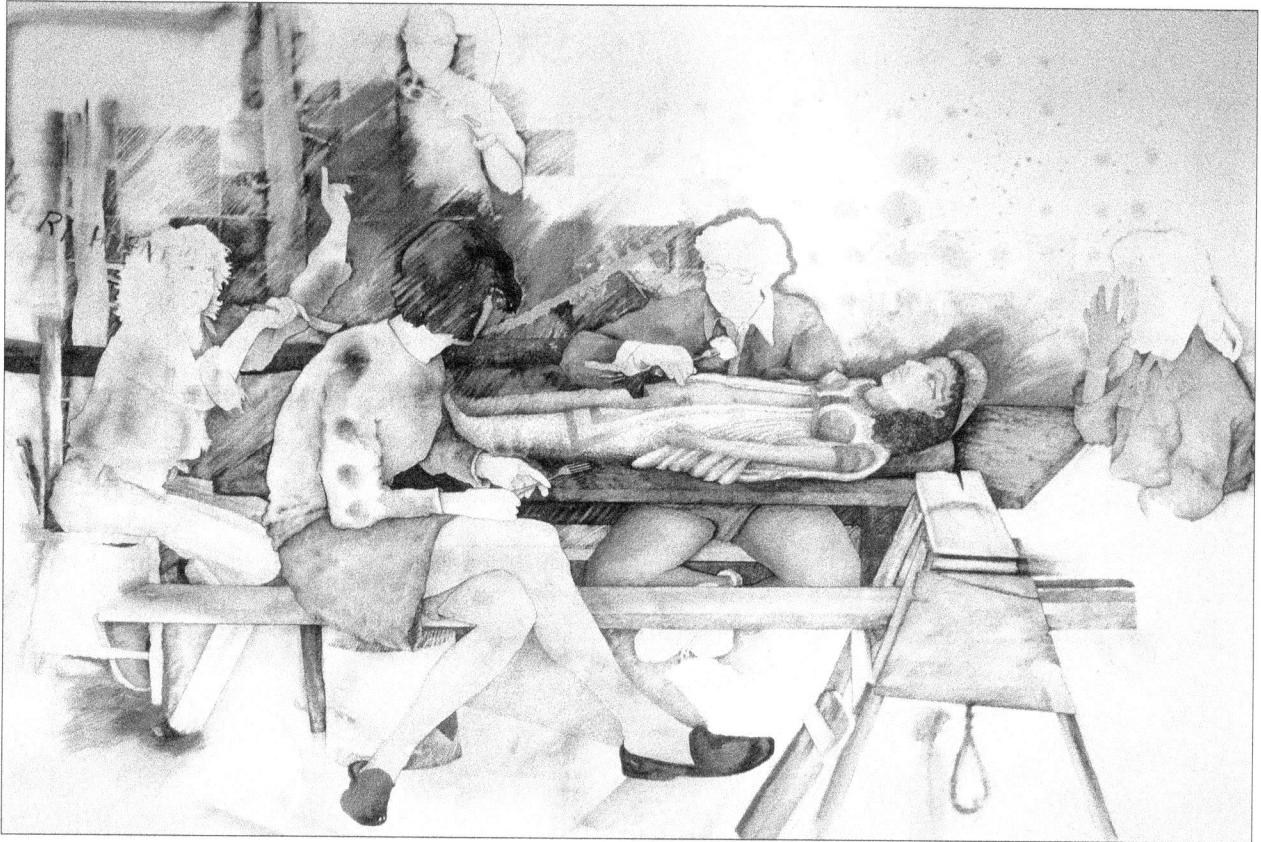

Judith Williams painting titled "Hunger " expresses the desire for culture as being the greatest hunger with the predominant group of artists that lived there full time in the 70's.

Pain Francais Et Mousse Au Chocolat

You may be surprised to find me included in this volume, thinking me only a gifted consumer of food—but as you will see your surprise is without foundation. Every Christmas at Refuge Cove found me taking Julia Child volume 2 from the shelf, turning to page 57 and slavishly following the 20 odd page recipe to produce the best bread ever eaten in Canada. I have had bread that tasted as good and perhaps looked marginally better but that was at the finest restaurant in France near Bordeaux—it had 3 stars from Michelin then in 1978 and still does to this day.

If you want to cause a sensation not to mention fighting and recrimination among your friends and acquaintance just follow the recipe and set the result on a table. I don't believe much of my bread ever made it to Christmas dinner proper as competition to obtain more than a fair share led to astounding behavior from the entire Refuge Cove population, even the mildest and most self effacing of our membership. Think of a cross between a heavy metal mesh pit (whatever the fuck that is) and the Ultimate Fighting Championship and your imagining is not far off.

Bobo's Version

(continued on next page)

Pain Francais Et Mousse
Au Chocolat

(continued)

Volume 1 of Julia Child at page 604 has a recipe for chocolate mousse. I made same for the first and as far as I know, the last of the Refuge Cove mousse-offs. This was an event in which a number of Refugees produced different versions of one of the classic French desserts to be judged for merit at an evening social event at the Cove. There were I think about 10 mousse on offer and prizes were awarded (bragging rights actually) for the best of them. Adding evidence for the truth of the old saw that there ain't no justice is the fact that my mousse did not rate highly—except of course among the truly knowledgeable (thank you Judy, Kathy and Inez). Unchocolatey, over sweet confections carried the day to the lasting shame of our small community.

Two hints for a successful mousse—I prefer Cointreau to Grand Marnier in the recipe. Also be warned that on another occasion I wanted to make mousse for dessert at a dinner party we were hosting. The recipe calls for beaten egg whites as well as yolks. Norm and Denise had ducks at the time so in experimental mode I thought to use eggs from these ducks. You can beat or whip the whites of duck eggs for a long time (I did) and nothing happens to them. They do not change and are therefore unsuitable for the purpose.

To fill up some more blank space I can think of two stories which I think cast me in a favourable light. The first concerns fish and chips while the second involves greed, injustice and Bud's goose.

Lisa G approached me when she was 12 or 13 and told me that she could eat more of Auntie Doris'

famous fish and chips (recipe can be found elsewhere in this volume) than I could.

An amazing claim from a demure young lady especially considering that I was and still am viewed correctly by my acquaintance as a prodigious eater—save Wilt Chamberlain I feared no appetite at table and I was in my greedy prime having recently won a free dinner at Monty's rib house in Vancouver by consuming 5 pounds of steak at one dinner sitting in their restaurant. So next fish and chip night we all gathered at Doris for what some imagined would be a contest. Lisa proceeded to amaze me and the rest of the assembled company by consuming piece after piece of Doris' wonderful battered red snapper. There is some disagreement about the number of fish she ate—some say 13 and she herself at this 30 year remove thinks the number was 15—no matter it was an astounding feat for a young female not much above 5 feet tall who in no way could be considered overweight. I was dumbfounded and so upset that I, unconsciously I now think, ate 24 pieces of fish worried that there would not be enough fish for me. She now claims she could have done more but that I would not let her near the table. I think I was concerned about the effects of so much fried fish on such a young, promising but inexperienced trencher person and I had been informed by the parental unit (hers not mine) that if she got sick I would hear about it.

Bud Jarvis kept geese at Tiber Bay. One Christmas the Refuge party planners decided that turkey was off for that particular year and that goose was the thing. Bud said he would bring a goose and two other geese were acquired commercially.

My Judy decided that the three geese should be stuffed with prunes which themselves had been larded with pate and that she would cook the same at Doris' on Christmas day. On arrival chez Doris we saw that the 2 commercial geese presented very well but that bud's goose looked a poor thing in comparison—undernourished and with a wrinkled skin. Judy put them in the oven and decided to take Bud's goose out earlier as it was smaller.

I should say now that I had been trusted to choose the wine for Christmas dinner and had chosen a number of bottles of Spatlese, a high end very slightly sweet German white wine which I was looking forward to. I saw Judy take the little goose from the oven and set it to rest and I must say it looked better than I had thought it would but we were not that hopeful. 10 minutes of the usual Christmas banter passed and I saw Judy approach the resting bird and take an exploratory piece of it into her mouth. A strange look clouded her visage; not one I had seen before as it was kind of sly. She picked up the platter and hastened into Doris' bedroom followed by the senior Gibbons, Bud and myself all of us thinking this was prelude to culinary disaster and that Judy was going to pitch the bird into the creek seeing as it was a complete failure. She however said something like "taste this and tell me I am crazy" We did and discovered the bird was beyond praise—ecstasy. I rushed to open a couple of bottles of the wine and the five of us devoured the bird and the wine out of sight of the assembled partiers. An orgy of greed of which I was a proud part of. I still believe that this was the best food and wine pairing I have ever encountered. The incident may also explain why none of the five of us was mentioned in Doris' will since even as hostess she got not a sniff.

I will leave others to tell the stories of Cadis' turkey moutarde en croute and Monika's Mink Island sliding turkey.

Bon Appétit,
Bobo Fraser

95

Almond Crescents

2 cups whole **almonds**

1 1/4 cup **flour**

1/4 cup **sugar**

1 cup **butter**

1 tsp **vanilla**

1 cup powdered **sugar**

Grind almond finely.

Set aside 1/3 cup.

Mix flour, sugar and remaining almonds, then butter and vanilla until mixture forms a ball leaving the sides of the bowl.

Chill 1 hour.

Form into crescents or any shape you want.

Press remaining almonds on top.

Bake at 350°F for 12–15 minutes on ungreased cookie sheet.

Dust with powdered icing sugar.

Lizette Beauchemin

Lemon Loaf

1 1/2 cup **flour**

1/2 tsp **baking soda**

1/2 tsp **baking powder**

1/2 tsp **salt**

3 **eggs**

1 cup **sugar**

2 tbsp **butter** softened.

1 tsp **vanilla**

1 tsp **lemon extract**

1/3 cup **lemon juice**

1/2 cup **coconut oil**

LEMON ICING

1 cup and 1 tbsp **powdered sugar**

2 tbsp **whole milk**

1/2 tsp **lemon extract**

Combine flour, baking soda, baking powder and salt in a bowl.

Use a mixer to blend together the eggs, sugar, butter, vanilla, lemon extract and lemon juice in a medium bowl.

Pour wet ingredient into the dry ingredients and blend until smooth.

Add oil and mix well.

Pour batter into a well greased 9x5-inch loaf pan.

Bake at 350 degrees for 45 minutes or until a toothpick stuck into center of the cake comes out.

Jen's Oatmeal Cookies:

For Denise & Pat

½ c. margarine
½ c. brown sugar   } Cream together

Add { 4 tbsp. boiling water + 1 tsp. Vanilla

Next { 3¼ c. oatmeal
Add { 1 c. coconut

1 c. flour
½ tsp. soda + ½ tsp salt   } Sift together
                              + add last

Drop by spoonful + press c fork dipped in milk.
Bake @ 350° for 10 mins. or so ~ watch close.

Carol Emmons recipe 1973
Oatmeal Cookies.

Archive photo "The Hole".

97

Cookies

1½ cups flour
2 teaspoons Baking Powder
¼ " Soda
¼ " Salt
½ cup soft shortening
1 cup white sugar
1 egg
1 cup crushed pineapple (drained)
¼ cup pineapple juice
1½ cups rolled oats

MRS. DOROTHY THOMAS,
REFUGE COVE,
B.C.

"Dorothy made her own kerosene logs by rolling the newspaper tightly tying it with string and soaking it in kerosene. She swore these were the best for heating. In 2-3 minutes a pot of water would be boiling on the stovetop."

Don Wicks

Oil Cookies, good

1 egg, beat slightly with fork, add
½ cup oil
¼ cup white sugar
" " Brown
1 Teaspoon Vanilla,
1 cup flour, 2 tsp. b powder
½ tsp salt. 1 cup rolled oats
½ cup coconut. Mix in order
given. bake about 8-10 mins

98

Homemade Ice Cream

I brought this recipe with me from Alaska originating from the Gustavus Inn. Since it is made from evaporated milk (canned cow) it is inexpensive and not too rich.

In a large mixing bowl break
5 **eggs** and beat them until they are thick and frothy.
Add 4 cans of evaporated **milk**
1 milk can of cold **water**
2 cups of **sugar**
1/2 te aspoon of **salt**
4 tbsp. **vanilla**

Mix well and pour into the can of your Ice cream freezer. Follow the manufacturers directions for freezing.

- *You can pour the mixture in a steel bowl and freeze it then scrape the frozen cream and whip it a few times.*
- *Use a hand beater or an electric mixer if you have power.*

Mary Ruzich

Mary.

Ariel & Alden.

Pat Lovell. 1993.

Photo courtesy of Lena & Mel

At the fish cleaning station. 1984.

Photo Frieda Home

CHRISTMAS RUM Balls

12 oz Semi Sweet **choco chips** (melted)

1 ½ cup **almond** paste

1 cup **sour cream**

Pinch **salt**

8 cups vanilla **wafers** crushed finely

3 cups **icing sugar**

1 ½ cup melted **butter**

CHOCOLATE SHOT

⅔ cup **cocoa**

⅓ cup white **rum**

2 cups **pecans** chopped fine

Mix these together to make shot.

Combine and cream well melted chocolate chips, sour cream, almond paste, salt. Set aside.

In separate bowl combine wafers and rest of ingredients except chocolate shot. Mix until it holds a ball shape. Add chocolate sour cream mixture. Knead with hands until blended and soft. Refrigerate until firm enough to hold shape but soft enough to pick up shot.

Roll smallish balls in pecans and place on trays with waxed paper under. Refrigerate when firm Put into tins and keep cold for up to 4 weeks. If kept longer freeze. Bring out into warmer room an hour before serving.

Pat Lovell

Photos courtesy of Frieda Home

BEST Banana Bread

Bake @ 350°F for 1 1/2 hours

3/4 cup **margarine**

1 1/2 cups white **sugar**

2 **eggs**

2 cups **flour**

1 tsp **soda**

1 tsp **salt**

1 1/2 cups mashed **bananas**

1/2 cups **buttermilk**

1/2 cup chopped **walnuts**

Cream margarine, sugar, and eggs.

Add banana's then flour, salt, soda alternately with buttermilk.

I use regular milk to which I add vinegar to make sour milk.

Blend well & pour into a greased bread pan.

Barbara made this recipe of banana bread, three loaves at time.

She bought the bananas from the store a case at a time.

In her letter she wrote: Seems if my memory serves me right that 4 1/2 cups mashed bananas filled an empty cool whip container.

I'd do the whole case and freeze them.

They were sold in the store by the half loaf for $4.50.

I also baked sticky buns for Reinhold to sell at the hamburger stand.

These were made with Bisquick.

I always wondered why I was never questioned at the border over my 2 dozen boxes of Bisquick!

Didn't really have a recipe for them—just like cinnamon rolls except with brown sugar.

They were very popular.

Some mornings I'd bake 6 dozen.

I also made dried apricot, zucchini and chocolate chip chocolate banana bread.

Barbara B. Emry

"Barbara and Lew first came to Refuge Cove on their live aboard boat Splink in 1976 and every year after until Lew passed away in 1985.

The next nine years Barbara drove up and lived in the boardwalk cabin or at Don Wicks home while he was away fishing. Some of her happiest times were spent at Refuge Cove with the original owners."

Barbara B. Emry

The Official Recipe for Banana Fosters

1/3 cup light brown **sugar**

1 teaspoon **cinnamon**

1/4 cup unsalted **butter**

1/4 cup **banana liqueur**

1/2 cup dark fighting **rum**

4 **bananas** halved lengthwise

vanilla **ice-cream**

1 small fire extinguisher

Melt butter in a heavy skillet using a medium flame.

Add sugar, cinnamon banana liqueur, ¼ cup of rum

Cook on low heat stirring until syrupy about 5 minutes.

Add bananas then coat with syrup, add remaining rum IGNITE!

Top with ice-cream. Pour the rest of the syrup over the ice-cream.

One less secret in the Universe!
Scott Rempe

"What to do with ripe bananas that you are unable to make a bread or cake with.

Peel and cut banana lengthwise laying out on wax paper in the hot sun to dry out.

If it rains put inside and keep drying them out until the sugars intensify.

Rolled in a banana leaf it lasts for days as a tasty sweet treat."

Carolynne Dove IV

from her family novel

"Seven Year Odessey"

Cocoa Fudge

3 cups **sugar**

⅔ cup **cocoa**

⅛ tsp **salt**

1 ½ cups **milk**

¼ cup **butter**

1 tsp vanilla

⅔ cup **pecan** or **walnut** pieces

Combine sugar, cocoa and salt in heavy saucepan.

Add milk. Bring to a boil, stirring until sugar is dissolved.

Do not stir again. Cover and cook one minute.

Uncover and cook to soft ball stage (238°F)

Add butter.

Place in a pan of cold water to cool quickly to lukewarm.

Add vanilla. Beat until creamy and candy losses its gloss.

Quickly stir in nuts and pour into buttered 9 inch square pan.

When firm cut into squares.

Dorothy Nelson

Dinner party gathering at Barry's place.

Photo by C J Campbell

"Dorothy Nelson gave me this recipe She was a boater who came every summer. She always had the fudge and Divinity aboard and was always passing it out. I could never make it as good."

Denise Gibbons

Divinity

2 1/2 cups **sugar**

1/2 cup light **corn syrup**

1/2 cup **water**

1/4 teaspoon **salt**

2 **egg whites**

1 teaspoon **vanilla**

1/2 cup chopped **pecans** (optional) or 1/2 cup **cherries** (optional)

1. In a 2 quart saucepan combine sugar, corn syrup, water, and salt.

2. Cook to hardball stage, (260 degrees), stirring only until sugar dissolves.

3. Meanwhile, as temperature of syrup reaches 250 degrees, beat egg white till stiff peaks form.

4. When syrup reaches 260°, very gradually add the syrup to egg whites, beating at high speed with electric mixer.

5. Add vanilla and beat until candy holds its shape, 4-5 minutes. Stir in the chopped nuts or cherries, if desired.

6. Quickly drop candy from a teaspoon onto waxed paper, swirling the top of each.

Bliss Balls

Get your morning going with this energizing and healthy brain food.

- **candied ginger**
- **raisins, currants**
- **dried cranberries**
- **chocolate chips**
- **ground walnuts, almonds**
- **cardamom**
- **coffee ground**
- **coconut**
- **ground flax**
- **sesame seeds**
- **sunflower seeds**
- **honey** or **maple syrup**
- **molasses**

Pulse in a food processor until all the ingredients formed together into a ball.

Remove and form into 2 inch balls.

Roll in coconut slivers or sesame seeds.

Keep cool.

100% dairy free / gluten free.

Homemade Yoghurt

High protein energy! Takes 6-10 hours to jell. If you don't appreciate the taste of "canned cow" add fresh fruit or jelly or jam.

- 1 cup "canned cow" **evaporated milk** 250 ml
- 1 cup instant **skim milk powder** 250 ml
- 3 cups medium—warm **water** 750 ml
- 3 heaping dessert spoons of any commercial brand of **plain yogurt** 25 ml

This is a *"culture base"* for the homemade stuff.

Combine all ingredients in a large bow.

Beat and stir well.

Pour into large crockery bowl and cover.

Set in a warm place, not a hot place.

Let set until thick 6-10 hours usually then chill.

Or add jello stir well to dissolve, let it set thirty minutes longer and then chill.

This recipe makes 4 cups.

Top with homemade granola.

Cathy Campbell

Mary Ruzich calls herself a gypsy quilter. She is an acclaimed intuitive designer and passionate hand-dyer. Color is her vehicle and textiles are her highway. Journey together with her through the fibers of imagination and creativity on her site, "Dye me to the Moon".

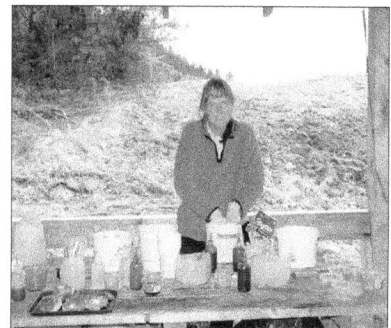

Mary giving a fabric dying workshop at the gazebo.

Blueberry Avocado Smoothie

Serves 2

- ½ cup frozen **blueberries**
- 1 cup **almond hemp coconut** or **rice milk**
- ½ **avocado**
- 1 cup chopped **fresh kale**
- 2 **dates** coarsely chopped
- 2 tbsp **hemp seeds**
- 1 scoop **protein powder** (optional)

Three Layer Lemon Pie

Rene has been making these famous pies for years for the potlucks at Refuge Cove. We always look forward to her pies as she usually makes two or more. Sometimes we have the pie first before dinner so that we can get a piece!

Bake a single pie crust and let it cool.

In a saucepan mix 2 slightly beaten **eggs yolks**, 1/3 cup **cold water** and 1 pkg of **lemon pie mix**.

Add 2 cup **boiling water**.

Cook over medium heat stirring constantly.

When bubbles continue to break the surface boil for 30 seconds longer.

Remove from heat. Stir in 1 tbsp **butter**.

Cool for 5 minutes, stirring twice.

Pour approx. 1/2 of **lemon mix** into cooled pie shell.

Beat **eggs whites** (no sugar necessary) until stiff then add the remaining pie filling to it and stir until completely blended.

This is the second layer.

Pour over first layer then let set.

The third layer is **whipping cream**.

You can add this as you serve it.

The spray type whipping cream works well.

Enjoy!

Rene Gay (M.V. My Happiness)

Balsamic Blackberry Crumble

Juicy blackberries picked from August to October can make many pies.

Preheat oven to 400°F

    2-3 freshly picked **apples** chopped up

    4 cups of fresh **blackberries**

    2 tbsp **balsamic vinegar**

    1 large handful of fresh gently separated **basil leaves**

    !/2 cup of Hoge's **honey**

Sprinkle top with mixture of:

    10 tbsp of **flour**

    5 tbsp brown **sugar**

    1 stick of **butter** crumbled

    Cinnamon

Bake for 30 minutes.

    Cathy

"Hanne was always very generous to me by reserving her blackberry bush. She knew I would be making many pies. I picked blackberries every other day until I had buckets of them then I made blackberry pies and crumbles for dinner parties and the late summer potlucks at the gazebo.

Results of an afternoon of baking pies in Hanne's kitchen, many pies, but never too many. The are always gone!"

Cathy Campbell

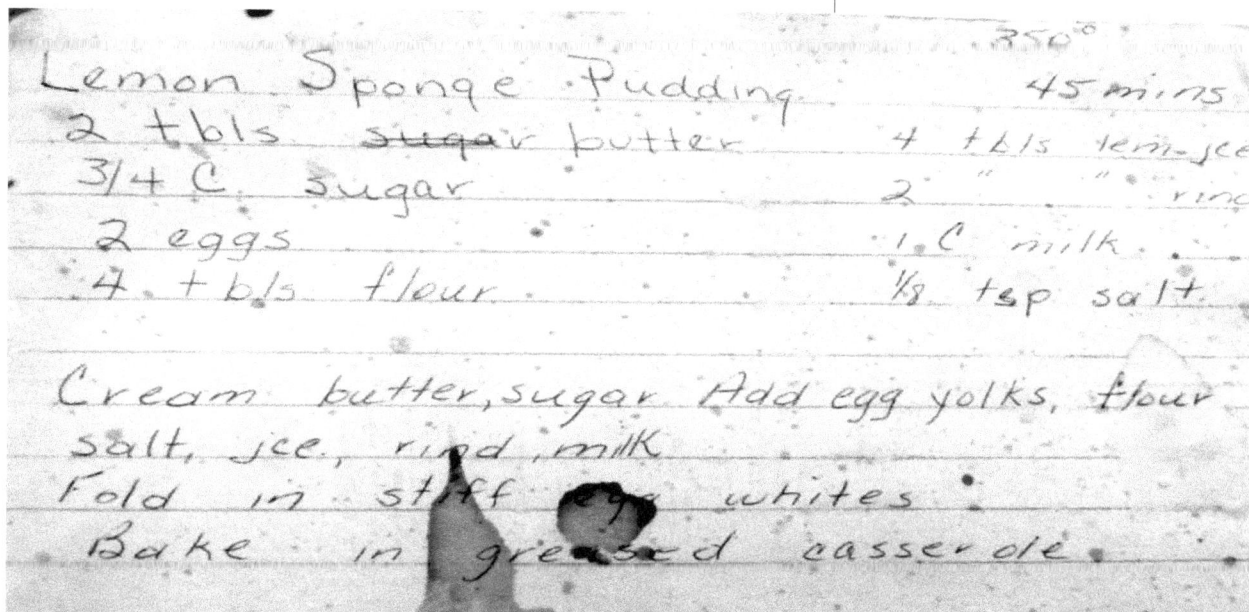

Lemon Sponge Pudding — 350° — 45 mins
2 tbls butter — 4 tbls lem-jce
3/4 C. sugar — 2 " " rind
2 eggs — 1 C. milk
4 tbls flour — 1/8 tsp salt

Cream butter, sugar. Add egg yolks, flour, salt, jce, rind, milk
Fold in stiff egg whites
Bake in greased casserole

This recipe was from B.C. Electric recipe booklets from the 50's.
Denise's mom made it as she was growing up.

Chocolate Avocado Pudding

In a processor, combine

    3 **avocados**

    1/2 cup **cocoa powder**

    1/2 cup **milk**

    1/3 cup **maple syrup** and

    1/2 tsp **vanilla**

Process and refrigerate until firm.

Fresh sun dried clothes hanging on the line at the Refuge Cove dock.

Raisin Pie

    2 cups **raisins**

    1 cup boiling **water**

    1 cup **brown sugar**

    4 tbsp **flour**

    1/4 tsp **salt**

    2 tbsp **lemon juice**

    2 tbsp **butter**

Simmer the raisins and water together over low heat for 5 minutes.

Mix the sugar and flour together.

Stir into the cooked raisins.

Cook until thick.

Add salt, lemon juice and butter.

Pour the filling into a pie shell.

Makes 2 pies.

Janet Ellis

Huckleberry Pie

Fresh Fruit in a Baked Shell....pie shell that is...

- 1 qt **berries**
- ¾ cup **sugar**
- ½ cup **water**
- pinch **salt**
- 1 ½ tbsp **cornstarch**
- 2 tbsp cold **water**

Boil sugar, water and salt until sugar dissolves.

Mix cornstarch and cold water.

Add to Syrup and 1 cup of crushed fruit.

Cook until clear and thick.

Place remaining fruit in baked shell and cover with slightly cooled sauce.

Top with whipped cream.

(I use less sugar, and it seems to work fine.)

Beth Hill

Beth Hill is the author of *Upcoast Summers, Seven Knot Summers, Petroglyphs of the Pacific Northwest, The Remarkable World of Frances Barkley, 1769-1845* and four other books.

Her family carries on the tradition of Refuge Cove living.

Picnics & gatherings were usually the grand outcome from a summer day combined with fishing and berry picking to make pies for desserts.
A feast at the Hill's outdoor kitchen.

Photo Courtesy of Frieda Home

Fruit Cobbler

J ust about any kind of fruit can be used for this cobbler black-berries, peaches, pears, thin apple slices over blueberries, blueberries with prune plum halves.

Arrange fruit in a shallow buttered baking dish not quite to the top.

Sprinkle with honey or sugar.

Topping – Cream 4 tbsp butter with 1/3 cup sugar. Beat in one egg and 2/3 cup mascarpone cheese. Add a splash of vanilla or almond extract. Stir in 2 tbsp flour.

Spoon over fruit.

Bake at 350°F for 20 minutes.

Dot with small chunks of Belgium chocolate and almond paste before spooning mascarpone mixture on top.

Cathy Campbell

Corrine & Spencer in her kitchen.

Haven Blue made this lattice topped blackberry after picking the blackberries ripened at Catherine's in late August 2001

Butter Tarts

Preheat oven to 375°F.

    1 cup **brown sugar**

    1 cup **raisins**

    2 **eggs**

    1 tsp **vanilla**

    1/3 cup **butter**

    4 tbsp **cream** or **milk**

    1/2 cup **walnuts** or **pecans**

    unbaked tart shells

Beat eggs.

Combine with remaining ingredients except nuts.

Boil at medium heat for 3 minutes.

Add nuts.

Fill unbaked tart shells.

Bake for 15 minutes at 375°F

Lizette

Gingersnap Cookies

Jenny Nelson ran the store with husband James when the co-op first began.

Cinnamon Rolls

Bill Rendall at his floating cafe in Squirrel Cove.

The Best in the World from Alaska to the Panama Canal! (makes 40)

½ cup **white sugar**

1 **egg**

1 cup **oil**

¼ cup **lemon juice**

8 cups Earl Grey **tea**

5 cups **flour**

4 tbsp **yeast**

8 tsp **salt**

12 cups **flour**

vanilla and **rum**

Mix first 7 ingredients together to make sponge. Let rise in warm place for one hour or until double. Add salt and remainder of flour and knead to a smooth dough. Let dough rise until double. Roll out into rectangle approx. 8" wide 12" long, and 1/8" thick. Can experiment with this according to how large you want the rolls.

Spread **butter** on rectangle. Sprinkle with generous amount of **cinnamon** and **brown sugar**. Add **raisins** and/or **walnuts** (optional). Roll into long cylinder and cut with sharp knife into 2" lengths. Grease baking pans and sprinkle generously with **brown sugar and cinnamon and cardamom**. Place rolls in the pan and let rise until double. Bake approx. 30 minutes in 375 F oven until nicely brown and cooked through.

Topping: Mix brown sugar, butter and a small amount of evaporated milk to spreading consistency. Add vanilla, rum extract or amaretto extract to mixture. Spread on warm buns when they come out of oven. You can experiment with the topping to suit your taste. Bill's favourite was the Rum! He had his bakery in Squirrel Cove and cruisers made a special trip to eat his delicious buns.

Julia & Ben Rendall

This Piñata party was at the Gibbons home.

Photo by Judith Williams

"Every New Years Eve Bill, brothers William, Christopher, Benjamin and I would go over to R.C in our boat, "S. Queen" and stay with Jerry White and Inez.

Dinner was at Bobo and Judy's home.

Judy made Piñata's and around midnight blindfolded the children and adults. With a broom we would try to break open the spinning piñatas.

Bottles of champagne were cooling in bathtub which was full of ice.

Ah, we had great New Year's memories."

Julia Rendall

It is a difficult task to grow fruit and vegetables for the lack of fertile soil. Years of composting and carting seaweed, starfish and soil from other areas has made it possible for some homesteaders to be self sufficient as far as vegetables go.

Mel star fishing for the garden. 1984

Putting the garden to bed. 1991

Photo of Lena taken by Mel Hart

SALAL PIE

Make it the same as blueberry pie, only put in lemon juice - say half a lemon per pie - plus a touch of cinnamon.

Tod

source: the Salal Authority of B.C.

Peaches with Ginger Preserve

Slice up peaches and add candied or fresh grated ginger, cloves, cinnamon, rice wine vinegar, pinch of salt.

Heat up on the stovetop until peaches are tender.

Carefully arrange in jar with juices, adding coloured peppercorns.

Keep cold and use within a week.

PRESERVES

Jam & Jelly

There are a lot of huckleberries to pick and the season is long. You just have to get to the berries before the forest creatures get them.

There are cherry trees also and elderberries. The cedar waxwings and yellow tanagers come in every year and feast on the berries. The cherries are picked usually every other year when the crop is more abundant.

Salal and Oregon Grapes aren't very easy to harvest on Redonda Island. There are never a lot of these berries and you have to work hard at it. There are always plenty of apples to compliment the jelly.

Crabapple Jelly with Liquid Pectin

3 quarts/3 liters fully ripe **crabapples**

6 1/2 cups/1600 ml **water**

2 tbsp/25 ml **lemon juice**

7 1/2/ 750 ml cups **sugar**

1 pouch **liquid fruit pectin**

Remove blossom and stem ends from crab apples. Cut in small pieces. Do not peel or core. Add 6 1/2 cups (1600 ml) water; bring to a boil and simmer, covered, 10 minutes. Thoroughly crush, then simmer, covered, 5 minutes longer.

Place in jelly cloth or bag and allow juice to drip through for a clear jelly. Squeeze out juice if you want more juice and don't care whether it is cloudy. Measure 5 cups (1200 ml) into a large saucepan. Add lemon juice. Add sugar to juice in saucepan; mix well.

Place over high heat and bring to a boil, stirring constantly. Immediately stir in liquid fruit pectin. Bring to a full rolling boil and boil hard 1 minute, stirring constantly.

Remove from heat, skim off foam with metal spoon. Pour quickly into warm sterilized jars. Seal while hot with 2 piece lids with new centers. Process 5 minutes in a boiling water bath. Begin processing time when water returns to the boil.

Makes about 9 cups (2250 ml).

Oregon Grape and Salal Berry Jelly

Enlist the help of guests to pick berries. Ray used to always say "a busy guest is a happy guest." Combine cleaned salal and Oregon Grapes in a large pot. I use a minimum of 3 cups Salal to 1 cup Oregon grapes to avoid using pectin, an ingredient that is not sold at the Refuge Cove Store. You can use more Oregon grapes or all Oregon grape for that matter, it's just that Salal berries on their own don't jell to jelly standards.

Add enough water to a large pot so that the berries just float. You've got about 10 cups of berries you'll be cooking it for at least 10 more minutes, maybe 20. Once you get the jelly to the point where it's dripping jelly like off the spoon give it a final test to check the consistency. Put a spoonful onto a saucer and freeze it for a couple minutes. When it comes out push it around with the spoon, it should look and feel just like jelly. Put it in jars, put the lids on, and admire the fruits of your labour.

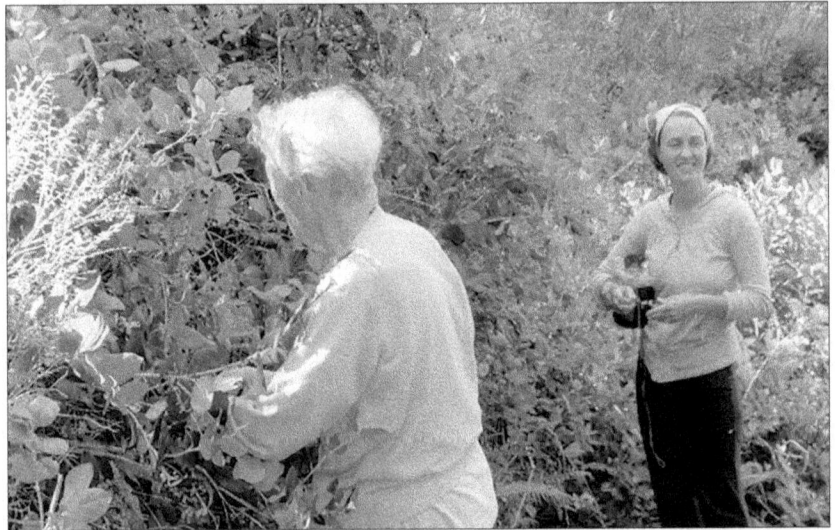

* If you want to make purely salal berry jelly for 1 qt of berries add 3 oz of pectin.

Cook over medium/high heat until berries are soft with Oregon grape it takes quite awhile.

Carefully transfer berries into a jelly bag, piece of cheese cloth or if you have neither a clean sock. Let the berries drip over night into a large pot or bowl.

Wake up, have breakfast, clear a space in the kitchen, then measure how much juice has accumulate in the bowl. Remember this number. Rummage around for enough jars and lids, sterilize them. Putting jars in a 200 degree oven is an easy way of avoiding having hot pots of boiling water around on a hot day.

Select a pot that's much bigger than you need. Bring juice to a full boil over high heat stirring a lot of the time. After it's boiled recall the amount of juice you measured and add the same amount of sugar.

Stir constantly now, bringing the spoon out from time to time to observe the change in the way the jelly runs off the spoon. At first it will drip quickly then it'll slow down into a slow stream/drip. Once you start noticing a scum on the top of the pot start skimming the scum off.

Just wanted to add a little after thought to my jelly recipe jelly. If it doesn't jell enough add some vodka to make a decadent liquor that's sure to be popular with your friends.

Sarah Kerman

PLUM CHUTNEY
3 # PRUNE PLUMS
1 # APPLES
2 BIG ONIONS
1 # BR. SUGAR
1 PINT DARK VINEGAR
1 OZ. ROOT GINGER (IN BAG)
1 TSP. CAYENNE PEPPER
1 OZ. WHOLE CLOVES (BAG)
1 TSP. SALT
BOIL TILL THICK — 2 HOURS

Balsamic Honey Jelly

1 cup **balsamic vinegar**

1 ½ tsp unflavoured **gelatin**

6 tbsp **honey**

In a small saucepan add vinegar & sprinkle gelatin over.

Wait 10 minutes until it is absorbed.

Stir over medium heat until dissolved.

Don't let it simmer.

Remove from heat and stir in honey.

Divide into small containers.

Chill until set.

Great served as a condiment or with bread and butter.

Cathy Campbell

Plum Chutney recipe.
Norm's mother started coming to
Refuge Cove in 1952.
She and Doris were great friends.

**Recollections from Denise
Gibbons**

Herb Cubes

Herbs preserved this way may be substituted for fresh herbs with little loss of flavour.

Basil, cilantro, tarragon, dill, lemon verbena any herbs will do.

Pack the fresh herbs in the bottom of sectioned ice cube tray. Pour water over herbs. Freeze. After frozen put in a sealed bag.

Beach Asparagus Pickles

5 quarts fresh beach **asparagus**

2 cups **onions**, sliced thin

1 **green pepper**, sliced thin

5 cups **vinegar**

5 cups **sugar**

1 1/2 tsp **turmeric**

1 tsp **cloves**

1 tsp **celery seed**

2 tsp **mustard seeds**

Pick over asparagus rinsing lightly. Do not soak.

Combine all ingredients in a pot and bring to the boiling point.

Pack in sterilized jars and process 10 minutes in boiling water bath or pressure cooker following instructions for canner.

Makes 8 pints. Best if left to sit for a month at least before opening.

Refuge Cove Kids. 2009. J. Frioud

DRINKS

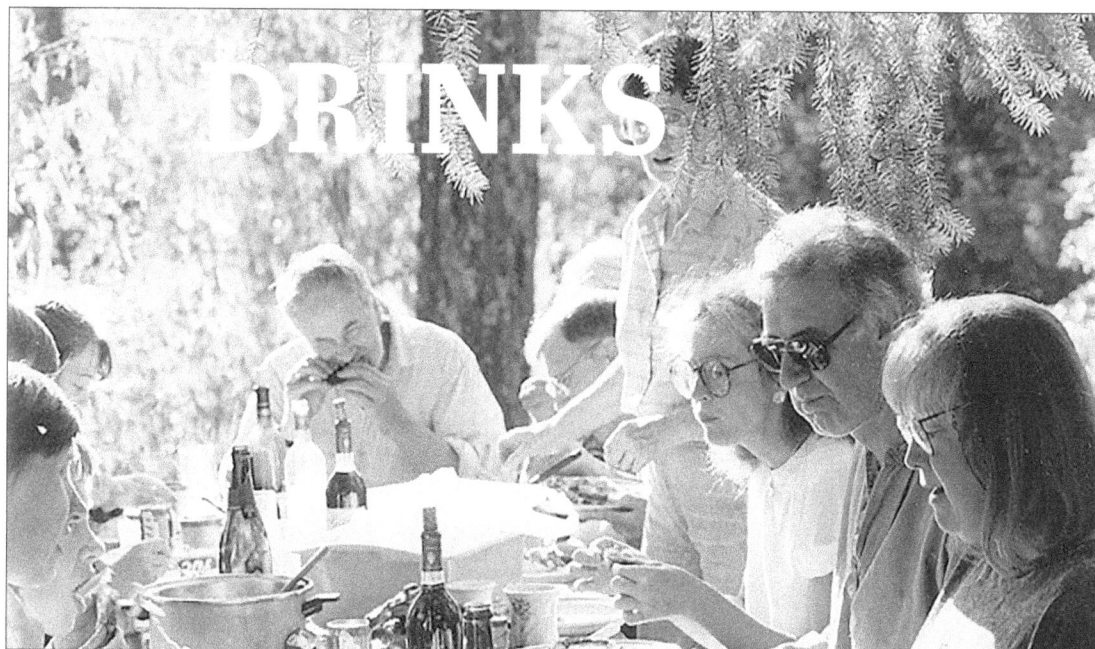

Dinner at Beth & Ray Hill's place.

Photo from Frieda Home

Salal Wine

4 lbs **salal berries**

1¾ lbs granulated **sugar**

6½ **pints water**

½ tsp acid blend

1 tsp pectic enzyme

1 crushed Campden tablet

1 tsp yeast nutrient

1 package **wine yeast**

Reinhold made Salal wine. People either loved it or absolutely hated it. Here is a recipe for Salal wine to try.

Put half the water on to boil and stir in sugar until dissolved.

Wash ripe berries. Mash berries in a cheesecloth bag.

Pour sugar-water over berries and add remaining water to help cool faster. Cover with another cloth and set aside until at room temperature. Stir in acid blend, yeast nutrient and crushed Campden.

Cover for 12 hours. Stir in pectic enzyme then recover and set aside another 12 hours. Add activated yeast and cover. Stir twice daily until fermentation dies down. Remove straining bag, squeeze to extract maximum juice, and discard pulp. Allow to settle overnight and rack into secondary.

Top up if required and fit airlock. Rack, top up and refit airlock after 60 days and again when wine clears.

Store in a cool, dark place for around 4 to 6 months, checking airlock periodically. Stabilize, sweeten to taste and set aside for 14 days.

Rack into bottles and enjoy.

Labrador Tea

Dry fresh leaves of this shrubby plants which is plentiful in moist areas in Desolation Sound.

Place in a shallow pan on top of the stove or in the oven at low heat.

When dry crumble them and use for tea. High in Vitamin C, it is reminiscent of oriental tea.

Ginger Wine

Fresh ginger chopped up and put in white wine or vodka or gin for a gingery flavoured drink.

Lavender Bliss

Lavender blossoms added to a bottle of gin or vodka and let it sit for a month.

Add some black current for a little sweetening and colour.

I added pineapple juice.

Make borage flower ice cubes for decoration in drinks.

Kahlua

4 cups of sugar

4 " " water.

1 bottle of rye

2 ounces instant coffee

2 (1') vanilla bean.

Bring water and sugar to a boil. Simmer 4 minutes. Dillute coffee with one cup of boiling sugar water. Bring to a boil again. Take off the heat. Add rye and vanilla bean(s) Let stand for 2 weeks.

Jenny Nelson's Kahlua recipe. She had a sake recipe that was also dynamite.

Denise

Blackberry Cordial

4 cups ripe **blackberries**

4 cups **sugar** or **honey**

Bottle of **vodka**

In a large bowl toss all together.

Cover with cloth and elastic band stir occasionally.

After three days add vodka and set in a dark place for three months just in time for Winter Solstice.

Strain into bottles. Mix with soda water.

Cathy Campbell

"Bobo would bring back apple cider from the Loon Ranch on Cortes Island. After many social hours of dining and drinks guests would depart from Mel and Lena's. Barry walked down the stiff leg on to the dock down to his boat and got home safely. Allen jump into his boat six feet shy of the dock and fell in, tipping his boat and Bobo rowed home."

Mel Hart

Raspberry Squash

Similar taste to kombucha

Apple cider vinegar

Raspberries

Cover them with apple cider vinegar. Let sit for a few days. Serve with sparkling water or ginger ale. Makes a very refreshing summer drink. Use other berries for this drink also.

Apple cider vinegar has been used for centuries as an energizing tonic and elixir.

Liz Cox Rogers

Happy hour is a very important daily ritual.

Saving the Songs of Innocence Blackfish

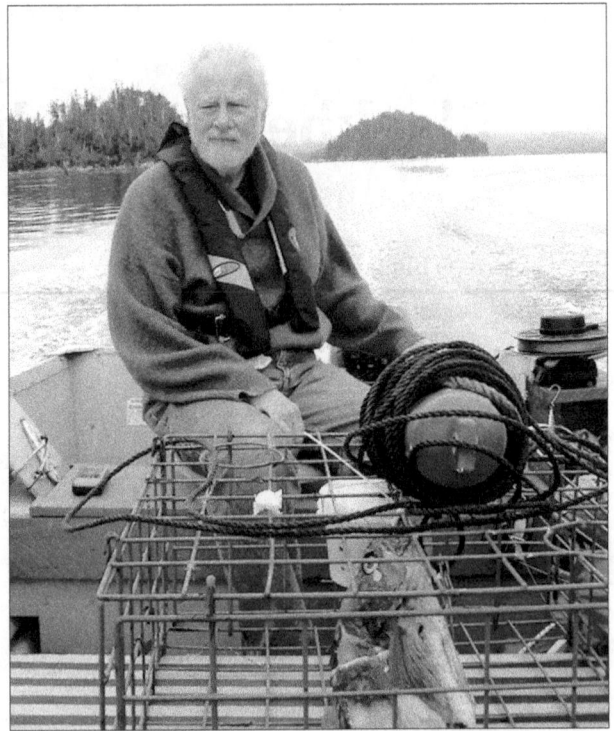

When I was a little boy, we called them Blackfish. My father and I would sometimes see them when we strip-cast for Coho at the mouth of the Big Qualicum River. We never got very close to them in that shallow bay, and I don't remember much more than the big dorsal fins coming up and going down in the distance – except that the fishing always seemed to go off then. Dad said that it was because the salmon hugged the bottom, dodging the hunting sonar of the Killer Whale pack. I still don't know if that's true.

Many summers later, with my own seven year old son, it was different. We were spinning for cutthroat at the mouth of a stream that flows into Pryce Channel, in the Desolation Sound area of B.C. It was hot, the deer flies were getting very tough, and we were starting to think more fondly of swimming than catching big trout.

"Puuuff." It sounded far away. But loud enough that we stood still in our little aluminum boat, watching in the direction of the Brem River.

In less than a minute, the black fin of a Killer slowly appeared about a quarter of a mile away. Edge on, it looked for all the world like a dock piling slowly wavering out of the water and then falling back in; except that pilings don't spout steamy breath. He was moving along the shore, coming out of Toba Inlet on a course that would bring him right up to us. His dorsal was so tall that it's tip drooped over in the way that (we say) means it's a big bull. Excitement! I started our old Evinrude and began idling along the shore waiting for him to catch up.

The next time he surfaced he was beside us, about thirty feet away on the open water side. I speeded up a bit to match his pace, and we held our course, staying about fifty feet off the steep shore. With not a ripple of wind on the water, we could see all of him as he angled into us a bit, coming up ten feet closer after his next short dive.

To say what is seen then is easier than to say what is felt or known. He looked like a huge rubbery thing that had been molded out of six or seven elephants. And I say "thing" because on one level he didn't appear, deliberately swimming at such profound ease, to be alive. Beside the obvious matter of the scale being all wrong, there was none of the fuss or busy-ness we associate with life, even when it is quietly on the move. But on another level, you didn't have to know that he ate seals like buttered popcorn in order to feel the near world humming with his predatory purpose. And we were alone with him – primates on a tin half-shell.

He went down again, shallow, and angled in another ten feet. When he came up we saw his eye, and Matthew said, simply and emphatically: "I'm scared now." "Smart," I said to myself: "You are being regarded by one who prefers dining as high up the food chain as possible." But out loud I did my father stuff: "We're okay. Let's just go along like this."

The tip of his dorsal slowly slid under again, and I watched it closely for any change of course. "Look!" Matthew yelled: "Look at the herring!" Under the boat I saw two things at once.

We had shall owed up so much that I could see the bottom about twenty feet down, and the boat was over a big school of herring packed against the shore. And then there was a different "PuuuuFF!" as the Killer surged up and dove, turning directly under the boat into the feed. I saw white and black under us and hit the gas. We squirted away, and turned around to look just as about 25 yards behind us, the whale erupted out of our wake.

He came out completely, but so slowly that it was hard to believe, from about the point he was halfway, that he could possibly go any further. And when he fell back into the light smoke of our exhaust, it seemed to take as long as the collapse of a dynamited skyscraper.

God knew what he was doing when he reminded a pushy Job that He was the creator of such as the whale. "And canst thou draw out his mouth with an hook?" After that, whether or not Job was satisfied with the all-mighty's account of his afflictions, the not-nearly-so-mighty them into perspective.

I tend to think of Job whenever I'm whacked over the head with a strong experience of nature. The story of his peek into God's wild portfolio, and his subsequent attitude-adjustment, reminds us of one of the rudiments of human wisdom: we are out of our depth in this world. In this respect, nothing has changed.

What has changed, sadly and urgently, is the gap between our relatively unimproved powers of understanding and the monstrous development of our capacity to despoil. I cannot really know the oceans that Homer called "the whale road", but I can effortlessly reach their deepest regions with a neoprene gumboot which has a half-life of about a million years.

But looking the whale in the eye with Matthew has produced at least one point of clarity in me. I don't know how I made my children, but I know that – in a way that has nothing to do with possession – they are mine and I must try to find the strength and wisdom to care for them. Now we know that we have mixed ourselves so completely with the world that not even the mercury and cadmium-laced flesh of the whales has been spared our touch. We have made ourselves so thoroughly immanent in the world that we have taken it away from nature and hence made it – if only through default – our own.

As is the case with God, when the wilderness no longer exists, it cannot be invented no matter how appealing the idea or powerful the human will to realize it. Because an invented God or an invented wilderness lacks the autonomous power that is at the core of its reality. Once innocence is lost, its songs can still be sung, but it can never be genuinely restored.

This means that the pious path of Job, leaving the running of the world to some separate and autonomous competence such as Spinoza's Deus sive Natura...God or Nature, is now forever closed to us. We never understood the significance of that path (the next best thing to not getting kicked out of the Garden of Eden in the first place) until it was too late, and now must search out a future of which the only thing certainly known is that it will require inestimably more from us than patient restraint. We face responsibilities, and obstacles in the way of their being met, of unfathomable profundity.

The good news – and it didn't have to work out this way – is that this wonderful world, as it reveals itself in Desolation Sound, continues to be as easily evocative of love as are our children.

John Dixon

"This was Cadi & Sherri's craft shop which was built in 1973, I think. We lived at the 'school house' which would have been directly to the right of this photo.

The Lovell family lived there one or two winters while we were in the school house."

Denise Gibbons

Photo Courtesy of Frieda Home. 1974

Pat Lovell and family lived in the Craft Shop for a year next to us at the old school house. She and Norm are cousins.

Photo from Mel Hart & Lena Johnson

Matt, Alister, and their mother Sandie owns and operates the restaurant and gallery.

Matt Dixon, entrepreneur, also designs furniture with Lifetime Timber. He cuts live edge slabs and large timbers reclaimed for use in furniture and post and beam construction.

2012 Refuge Cove Gallery & Upcoast Summer Restaurant above where the craft store once stood.

Barge Girls Dog BONeS

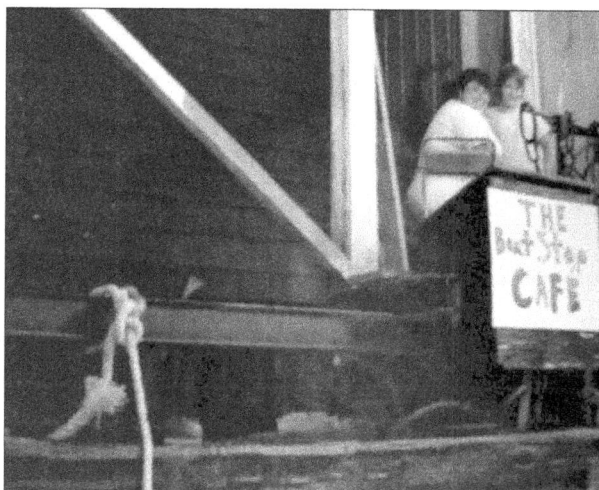

2 cups/500ml all-purpose **flour**

1 cup /250ml **cornmeal**

1/4 cup/50ml **wheat germ**

2 tsp/10ml **beef bouillon power**

1/2 tsp/2ml **Garlic powder**

1 large cooking **egg**

1 tbsp/15ml cooking **oil**

1 cup/250ml hot **water**

Preheat oven to 275°F combining first five ingredients in a bowl.

Add the egg, cooking oil, water. Stir well. Roll out onto a well floured surface until thickness is 1/2 inch.

Cut into bone shapes or others shapes. Arrange on a ungreased cookie sheet, Bake center rack for about 2 hours until dry and very hard. Cool. Let cookies stand overnight to dry thoroughly. Store in a container with a lid.

Makes 10 large bones or 14 puppy bones.

Myself I added different spices to it, and my dogs loved these very easy simple treats.

Carol O'Hara

"Dog Venison Miller Grub

Any trim off venison and fatty parts can go to the dog.

Can it up."

Don Wicks

Good Luck, Good Health, God bless you,
Is all that I can say.
G... L..., G..., H..., ...
When I am far away.
No matter where you wander
.. .. roam
Good Luck G. H. G. B. Y.
And bring you safely home.

Dorothy Thomas wrote this poem which I often have heard the boys at Refuge Cove recite softly and gently with great tenderness under their breath after being out on the water fishing or cruising. "Tell them I was Happy" is another endearing quote often said when departing.

Arriving home they are once again, as Don Wicks always says, "Safe in Camp."

Meghan Paterson came to Refuge Cove on a painting residency at the Refuge Cove Gallery. The collection of paintings, *Safe In Camp*, was inspired by the images of residents, buildings and boats at Refuge Cove.

Desolation Sound Detail

Mystery Reef
(FOUL AREA)

www.ingramcontent.com/pod-product-compliance
Lightning Source LLC
Chambersburg PA
CBHW081011040426
42443CB00016B/3486